Father Slavko Barbarić ∗ **PEARLS OF THE WOUNDED HEART**

INFORMATIVNI CENTAR

M E Đ U G O R J E

DIRECTOR:
Fr. Miljenko Stojić

EDITOR:
Krešimir Šego

CROATIAN ORGINAL TITLE:
Biseri ranjena srca

TRANSLATORS:
Schwanhild Heintschel - Heinegg
Rita Falsetto

LECTURERS AND PROOF READERS:
Rita Falsetto
Schwanhild Heintschel - Heinegg

© Župni ured Međugorje

CIP - Katalogizacija u publikaciji
Nacionalna i sveučilišna biblioteka, Zagreb
UDK 241.13
178

BARBARIĆ, Slavko
Pearls of the wounded heart / Slavko Barbarić;
(prijevod Rita Falsetto i Schwanhild Heintschel
- Heinegg); Zagreb;
Informativni centar Mir - Međugorje,
1998. - 214 str.; 20 cm
Prijevod naslova: Biseri ranjena srca

980227027

ISBN 980227027

Father Slavko Barbarić

PEARLS OF THE
WOUNDED HEART

MEĐUGORJE
1998.

I dedicate this book to all, who love, protect and save life. I pray to God, the Source of Life, with Mary, the Queen of Peace and the Mother of Life, for the conversion of all, who do not love, who do not protect, but destroy life.

The Author

TABLE OF CONTENTS

FOREWORD

This book is a touching testimony of the great epidemic of drug consumption, which is spreading more and more over the world, that endangers the physical, spiritual and mental structure of man and fatally threatens his biological existence. It is a particular illness of our civilization, the roots of which lie in the absence of God in human hearts, in society, in the family and the entire world. So the epic poem of materialistic atheism knocks against the wall and causes in many people, tragedies and dramas in thousands of acts.

This generation barely succeeds to recognize and admit that there are greater needs for man than a higher materialistic standard and that there are worse dangers than concentration camps and the hydrogen bomb. There is a greater need for the presence of God than for any other good. Drugs and Aids are even a worse evil than war. It was exactly the hunger for God that drove men to look for Him on their own; this, however, did not bring them to Him because they inexcusably mistook the Creator and creation. But from this result the worst consequences because they throw man, alongside the other evil, back into his original nothingness.

The rejection of God is at the same time the rejection of man, because man is the living image of God. That is why every atheism is, at the same time, anti-humanism.

Since the 19th century, we are witnessing this insanity, which is intensifying, and also the multiplication of its forms. The reign of irrationality based on this insanity causes a religious-cultural genocide, which today is being executed with our own human hand. The more insane it becomes, the more dangerous it is and thus surpasses each one before him.

Things cannot give what God can give. The mistake is fatal. Even more, not only in their inadequacy, things cannot give what they promise and what one expects from them, but they rob man of his freedom and make him a slave.

The addicts went out into the world in order to consume their worldly and physical passions with a substitute for God, which today calls itself 'drug'. The drug is an alternative for the mind and faith. This boundless consumption is really a boundless death, which through drug intake, is only being practiced better.

Parallel to this, poverty increases, especially the one of life, and darkness becomes more impenetrable, especially and mainly in the heads of men. Hearts are slowly being emptied and turn into garbage dumps, homes are being devastated and they turn into death tombs while the quality of life sinks and changes into senselessness. Not only the health of man, but also the existence of the nation and the Church are called into question since, because of drug consumption, they belong already today in the category for survival and tomorrow it will be even worse.

The drug recruits a dangerous army that storms against its own country. The most difficult and most necessary thing that we will be confronted with, is the alteration of man. But first he must be helped up. Everything else is easier: to renew and rebuild old villages, towns and factories. Despite all the difficulties, one must not overlook the renewal of man. Evil will not stop itself, neither stop to enlarge itself nor to multiply. In the fight against evil, there exist no helpless or uninvited at all. The true friend of man is the one who stands next to him when he is wrong. It is much easier to stand at his side when he is right.

We have opened our eyes to misfortunes, but not our hearts. The mere, obvious discard of humanitarian aid does not suffice even as an excuse. The indifference is a betrayal of man. One must not permit that the other has to carry his misfortune alone because this misfortune is not only his. After a correctly made diagnosis, one has to take up arms for the encounter with the drugs, as mighty and as resistent as they may be.

This is a situation which neither money nor intelligence can solve and endure, but only love. Sister Elvira has this love and that is why she has such immense successes, that neither a social nor a scientific institution can even closely attain. She recognized the root of the evil of drug addiction better than anyone else and only she opposed this evil with the only successful means-with faith and with love. The proclamation of general human principles does not solve concrete problems. All men are called upon and are able to love and God has engaged them to give His love to others and that is first to those, who are most in need of it. And who is more in need than the addicts, because they are poor in God and in life, and they are being robbed of their freedom, their humaneness and their inborn rights?

Humanity must not exhaust itself in moralizing, but must develop and take up the intiative and generate already existing structures in order to create a fuller life for those from whom it was taken, either through their own fault or the fault of others. For love, it is not important, who is guilty. It is important, who is more needy and who is really needy.

Any successful therapy must be preceeded by the correct diagnosis. The addicts are persons, who do not find God within themselves or believe Him to be irrelevant. This is also the reason for their unenviable situation. The problem of drugs can, therefore, not be solved either through psychology, psychiatry nor medicine and, therefore, can also not be healed with aspirin, pills, injections and surgical measures. Only faith can do that. This is why one should inject into addicts and into people in general, faith, that brings life and resurrection, instead of drugs, which bring death and destruction.

In harmony with this and, at the same time, as a confirmation, Sister Elvira discovered the diagnosis and treated the illness of drug intake from the right angle and the only successful method of healing. She recognized in this illness the absence of God and found the medicine in His presence in the empty, abandoned and wounded hearts. Therefore, she also did not seek help from doctors and psychiatrists but from God. She led her proteges not into hospitals but into 'cenacles', which she has orientated according to the wish of Our Lady of Medjugorje. This is exactly why she founded one of her numerous communities here and inscribes her proteges into the school of Mary, in which the subjects and the therapy are the messages of Our Lady: faith, conversion, prayer, fasting and-as the culmination-peace. All other diagnoses are wrong and the methods of healing, that correspond with them, are a type of 'placebo'.

The sensational success confirms the accuracy of this diagnosis and of the applied therapy. No other institution, neither a social nor a medical one, can boast with such successes as the 'cenacles' of Sister Elvira. In other modern institutions in the world, which care for addicts, there is scarcely 1% of healed addicts, whereas in the 'cenacles', at least the one in Medjugorje, there are 70% - 90% healed. Thus the messages of Our Lady of Medjugorje show which way mankind should take in order to liberate itself from the destruction, which threaten it with physical and spiritual prison. According to Mary's testimony and intercession, God bows down over graves and wasted away bones to enliven and save us.

In God's plans we must not place any 'buts' but an 'I believe'. Faith and love triumph over death and also over the death from drugs.

In every human being exists an everlasting future. One only has to liberate it through faith and love in oneself and the others. God's proposal exists also today and waits for the answer of faith so that resurrection can take place.

Medjugorje, April 1997.
Fra Ljudevit Rupčić

INTRODUCTION

When I listened to Sr. Elivira for the first time, it became clear as daylight to me, that the horrible monster of drugs extends its deathly claws toward innocent victims and mercilessly chases young lives and devours them.

This is surely not the first time that I encountered the problems of addicts, but Sr. Elvira's approach opened my eyes. I understood that many raise the white flag in front of this monster of drugs and other addictions and helplessly criticize authorities, the Church and the police for doing nothing. Sr. Elvira looked like a mother, a true descendant of Mary, the mother of the living, who fights for and redeems Her child, whom the dragon wants to devour. At the same time, I felt that many mothers and fathers have lost their courage and look on helplessly as their children become victims and lament over them, like Rachel lamented over her children, because she did not have them anymore.

While I felt the strength of motherly love in the gaze, the words and the deeds of Sr. Elvira, which prove her motherly love, I also felt the helplessness of many. While the motherly strength fails, that by its nature is always ready to protect life, I understood one truth:

THE DRUG IS NOT THE PROBLEM, THE PROBLEM IS THAT THERE ARE NOT ENOUGH ELVIRAS!

Mother Teresa of Calcutta once said, "What can the world expect today when the motherly hand has become the most dangerous murderer of life? How many innocent are being killed in the womb, in that space that God has created and given to man to cooperate with Him in the creation of life?"

That is why I don't find it an exaggeration to connect the helplessness over drugs with the willful killing of the unborn. The hand that kills her unborn child cannot protect her born child.

This book does not intend to condemn someone, but wants to describe Sr. Elvira's heroic deed, which in recent times has expanded unbelievably and has offered and is offering a secure place of refuge to hundreds of youths from all over the world. Thank God, her motherly hand has spread her activities from Italy to Croatia, France, Austria, Brazil and the USA.

I know many ask Sr. Elvira, like the Macedonians asked St. Paul, to come and proclaim redemption to them.

While it is the goal of this book, to bring closer to you, dear reader, the wonderful work of Sr. Elvira, may it awaken hope and love in you, which will be prepared to do something and, at least, to save one life. In case you don't know what you could do, it is not necessary to study or theoretically know all possible addictions, but it is enough **TO LOVE IN A MOTHERLY WAY, THEN LOVE WILL INSPIRE YOU IN THE RIGHT WAY, BECAUSE LOVE IS CREATIVE.**

The experience of Sr. Elvira can also help with theoretical knowledge in the treatment of addicts.

I give you this book in the hope that you will fall in love with life and protect it and so become a student of the Queen of Peace, the Mother of the Living. Dear reader, may these pages inspire you as a child of Mary to accept life, love and defend it!

There, where life is accepted and protected, there will also be PEACE.

I. THE PROBLEM
OF ADDICTION IN GENERAL

Man is a creature of God. According to His creation, man is limited. Although one speaks of freedom, it has to be emphasized that it is not absolute, in the sense, that man can do what he wants. The freedom of man is not only conditioned through his limitations, but also through experiences he carries in his soul, experiences with himself and with other people. The basic wish of every human being is to love and be loved, to have peace and to be happy. It is exactly here, however, that man meets his limitations and those of others. Man cannot love as he wants to, therefore, he also cannot be loved the way he wants to be. There is a deep layer in the human soul, in which exists this inability to love and so also an inability to be loved.

Our basic experience in the family, especially with the parents, is marked with this inability.

Since the parents are also limited and cannot love as they want to, there remains in each human soul a blank emptiness. But emptiness is always dangerous. Nature does not tolerate emptiness, said the ancient Latins. As much as parents try, they cannot love their child so much that, through this love, he will be happy and peaceful and will have no need to look for a substitute for love.

We simply say that God wanted it this way and look for Him continuously and in everything. This is how it really is. Man turns easily to other people and things and tries to compensate for this lack of being loved. This experience, where the love of others is limited, often creates a negative feeling of exclusion and non-acceptance and one easily begins to accuse them. But he, who accuses, does not love. He, who does not love, is open to all kinds of negative influences and quickly believes the easy promises to find love in their way.

He, who begins to fill his inner emptiness by turning his entire being towards God, will, in his inability to love, become more able to love unconditionally. The wounds, which remain in his soul because of not being loved, turn into the space and the reason for the love of God and the others. But when it happens-and it unfortunately happens often-that a man, because of an unfulfilled desire, turns towards himself, other people or things, he then slowly becomes an egotist and full of pride and tries to use everything in order to be happy.

In this struggle, he suppresses the others, gives them orders, conducts himself unfairly and even kills only for his well-being or he submits himself to others and becomes a slave, again because of his yearning to be happy.

Already the psalmist said that, the man, who relies on another man, is damned. Turning to another person in the yearning for love, always leaves wounds, in which bitterness develops and the sense for life, friendship and loyalty is lost. Man becomes unstable and his yearning continues. In this yearning, he is confronted with different offers and he becomes a slave. Thus, he becomes a slave of and dependent on material things, that give him a sense of contentment but kill him at the same time. It is enough to only think of alcohol, drugs, food, money, gambling and many other forms of addictions in order to understand the horror of addiction.

The sign of every addiction is that the person slowly loses his inner freedom and destroys himself or others, but most commonly he destroys himself as well as the others. Each type of addiction threatens the ability to love selflessly, to make sacrifices and to make the other happy and increases the spirit of distrust, lies, violence and unfairness. In the end, the person loses his standard for every value of human life and slowly loses respect for his own life. An addict knows neither father nor mother, neither brother nor sister, neither friend nor colleague; he then loses the sense for the value of the family, of prayer and of fasting. Everything becomes a means for his addiction. St. Paul said that for those who love God, everything will turn to good. So it is our hope, that we-even if it destroys us completely-can be resurrected.

From this view point, we can easily understand the wandering and searching of St. Augustine, who in one moment jubilated because he experienced love late and realized that God had created the human heart for Himself and that it is not at ease until it has found peace in God.

Surely, one finds this peacefulness in the God of love, in God, who loves us immensely. In Medjugorje, since the 2nd of August, 1987 on every second of the month, Our Lady prays with Mirjana Soldo for the unbelievers, meaning those, who have not yet experienced the love of God.

He, who experiences the love of God and whom it grasps, leaves everything with the power of the love that liberates and he will be able to become a human being, a child, a friend, a husband, a father and a brother to each person.

It is not worthy of a human being that the love for another person or for material things makes him a slave, an addict, or one, who, even though he has eyes, does not see and, even though he has ears, does not hear.

Therefore, the ideal education for every person is when his teacher, with his insufficient love, shows him the boundless love of God, which fills that emptiness in which nothing created-but only God-can enter. God brings peace and the capability to love and with this capacity to love, the joy returns into the human soul. This makes a man a man, but the addiction makes him a slave, a monster, an unhappy and violent person.

The hope that someone puts into people and things deceives and when hope deceives man, he will be disillusioned and becomes more open to the dangerous addictions, as far as self- destruction on the mental, spiritual and even the physical level is concerned.

The most beautiful experience a person can have is that he is being loved by God, the Creator, and that he can return this love to God and others.

While one talks much today about preventive measures, which are surely helpful, it is the best way to help people to get to know God's love, which loves him boundlessly and unconditionally. Negative experiences, however, very often become hinderances on this path.

Conditional love is dangerous, as it means being loved if one is good and successful; this love, that he has to earn, puts man under great pressure and so he always strives for it. So one becomes easily tired, gives up and turns to easy promises and true love remains unattainable for him.

That, which runs like a red thread through all the testimonies of the young people in the communities of Sr. Elvira, is the unconditional love for everyone who comes. This love returns to each person his feeling of self-worthiness, even if the person feels he is of little worth, but also if he has actively destroyed everything.

How many people drink, take drugs, gamble, stand night and day in front of slot machines just to have, for one moment, the feeling that they are somebody, know something, can do something to overcome their fears, their insecurity, their distrust and bitterness.

In the Holy Scriptures, God presents Himself in Jesus Christ as the One who is eternally in love with mankind. God searches for man, rejoices when He finds him, waits for him like the merciful father until man realizes that happiness lies in returning into the embrace of the father, from which he had fled, like breaking the chains that had bound him from living a life in freedom.

Only the divine sun can warm the depth of the human soul. Only the light of God can lighten and chase away the darkness of the human souls and hearts. Only God's trust for man heals the hearts from mistrust. Only the love of God enables man to lead a normal life with the others and to keep his inner freedom and joy.

II. THE COMMUNITY SPEAKS ABOUT SR. ELVIRA

It is always difficult to describe a person because it basically means that one enters into the true mystery of the Creator. But let us nevertheless try.

Since her childhood, Sister Elvira was educated and prepared for the mission, which she is fulfilling among the poor today. God alone prepared her for this. She was the fourth of seven children. Ever since she was small, she had to replace her mother, who was working in a hospital, while the father was serving in the military (it was the time during WWII). During that time, she took care of her brothers and sisters, the older as well as the younger ones. She had neither the time nor the chance to think of herself. It became natural for her to serve and serving became part of her nature; she owns nothing and spends no time for herself. This is why one should not be surprised that Rita (this was her name when she was small and it means "pearl") decided to enter the community of St. Joan Antida, as SISTER OF LOVE, whose charism is similar to that of Sr. Elvira. She took her fourth vow, to serve the poor, and she was given the name she carries today. The ethymological meaning of the name 'Elvira' is 'strong woman' and it is clear that nothing happens by chance to the one who loves.

The Lord knew that she would be a strong woman. A woman, who is determined, who fears no one or nothing, who does everything in order to help a brother in need, who does not fear criticism, the opinion of others and taking risks. She is a woman, whose only desire is to reach the 'kingdom of God', a woman who never says NO to anyone, who always

has an answer and, with a very sensitive soul that was created for love, stretches out her hand to all persons, who come to her for help. Decisive as she is, she accepts no compromises and half solutions and she is ready to squeeze everything out of a person, who needs to recognize the truth about himself. She is a woman, who can see the person entrusted to her with the eyes of God better than with her own, a woman who is never satisifed with the minimum when she recognizes the talents and possibilites in a person, but helps tirelessly so that everything can become a reality and everything possible is done. She is a woman, who is being lead and animated by LOVE alone - concrete, deep, true love, which life gives; the same that Christ asked from his disciples and that they could only give Him.

In the course of time, however, difficulties arose, but the Lord leads people and prepares them for great things. Everything that Sr. Elvira does today and that she is successful in doing is the fruit of numerous temptations, sorrows, humilitations and sacrifices and confirms everything that the word of God tells us: 'through the fire, gold is purified and people, through sorrows' and also 'if the grain of wheat does not die, it remains alone; however, if it dies, it bears rich fruit.' Today Sr. Elvira is the grain that has fallen upon the earth and thus becomes the food and life for many.

She had to wait many years to be able to build the house for the needy that she had first built in her soul. She waited for many years in faith and obedience for the answer from her community and these years of waiting served for her growth and purification of everything that was still human in her. We know that God is not in a hurry and that He leads his subjects.

In July 1983, at the age of 46, Sr. Elvira opened her first house. Because of the quick expansion of her work, it already became clear during the first four years that this work was the will of God, which He leads and Our Lady, Herself, defends and protects.

III. SR. ELVIRA'S EXPERIENCE - SR. ELVIRA SPEAKS ABOUT HERSELF

Sister Elvira, Rita Agnes Petrozzi, comes from a large fam-ily. She has five brothers and two sisters. Her father was an ordinary worker and her mother a housewife. Sr. Elvira fin-ished high school and at 19 years of age, she entered into a community, the Sisters of Love, that had been founded by Sr. Giovanna Antide Tournet. She lived in this community for 35 years and performed various duties. She got along well and was happy.

Let Sr. Elvira speak about herself:

"Something within me urged me continuously to dedicate myself to the poor of our times especially the young addicts, who also are our poorest contemporaries because they have no security, no family, no feeling of self-worthiness and no respect for others. They are the rejeced ones and, therefore, distrust everyone. Knowing all this, I often ask myself: How do we, the people of today, actually believe in God?! And what do we think when we utter big words like love, mercy, for-giveness, sacrifice - when the poorest among us cannot feel this at all?! When this question was occuppying me completely, I began to ask my superiors more often for permission to dedi-cate myself to these poor. However, during six years, this re-quest was refused 11 times because my superiors found that I did not have enough reasons for the service requested. How-ever, I waited patiently and was convinced that one day I would receive permission, if it was the will of God. Finally in 1983, I received it. At the same time, I was permitted to open the first house in Saluzzo near Torino."

Asked how one recognizes the will of God, Sr. Elvira answered:

"In order to recognize the will of God, one must first of all pray much. This is the means through which the Lord expresses His will. I also believe that we should never give our personal answers too early. The first sign that we act in accordance with the will of God, is the inner peace, the inner patience in awaiting the decisive answer.

So I acted, never, not for one moment, did I have any doubts about my future service, taking care of the poor - the addicts.

And I believe this love was conceived in the family. My father was inclined to drink alcohol so that already as a child I felt ashamed and was humilitated because of this. As I was standing next to his deathbed, as a mature person, I thanked God for such a father. Because, had he not been so, such a love and affection for all other addictions would probably not have developed . . ."

While many addicts justify their behavior and their addiction with the problems in the family, Sr. Elvira said:

"In my case, it was the other way around. It was exactly out of the situation in the family, that a special love for the addicted and a fiery desire to dedicate myself to their healing and spiritual change was born. In addition, it is known that many people, who have addicts in the family, show embarassment and shame. I must admit that I have learned what is meant when it is said in the Holy Scriptures that for those who love God, everything will turn to good. I love God, I have forgiven my father and, as I forgave him, I began to love him. Now I know that, through his sorrows, my service was born. I am very thankful to God because everything is being transformed into good."

When questioned how she came to Medjugorje, Sr. Elvira answered:

"In 1983, our community was founded and I came for the first time to Medjugorje in 1985. Before that, I had read about it and heard testimonies about spiritual experiences in Medjugorje and, therefore, wanted to bring some members of my new community with me on my first pilgrimage to Our Lady in Medjugorje. This I made a reality. Upon arrival in Medjugorje, we met the visionaries, Vicka and Marija. They were very open and this was especially important for us. The following year, I came again with a group and we remained 40 days. We had many difficulties with the police, but we remained steadfast. Why I liked to come here, what has kept me here and induced me to open a house for former addicts in Bijakovići, is mainly the fact that the prayer of everyone of my young boys and of the entire community became stronger and deeper here. Among other things, we have strengthened the spirit of our prayer and began to read the Holy Scriptures more often and more concentrated. My boys have really changed for the better in every way. This is why the following year we remained six months in Bijakovići. Again we had difficulties with the police, but Our Lady protected us during the whole time. After all the experiences, we all came to the conclusion that we had found a new country here, exactly the right spiritual refuge for addicts. How could it be different when our heavenly Mother is with us, whose presence we feel so strongly!! Therefore, it is not surprising that our youths simply do not want to leave, although they have better living conditions in Italy than here. They really long for God and here they quiet this longing better than anywhere else. I must say, it is here that they receive more easily the motivation for healing and this is why they are being healed earlier."

When I asked her if she would like to give a message to us all, she said:

"I am not a scholar so I also don't have an important message. But one thing I do know — The Mother and the Virgin is active here and is an inexhaustible fountain of evangelizing stimulation for giving birth to and protecting healthy offspring and healthy youth. This is why the parents and their children should, in the most spiritual way, make use of the presence of Our Lady in this area. The parents, by leading an exemplary Christian life, not only give birth to their children physically but spiritually and resuscitate them again and again, and the children, by following their spiritual examples, recognize that a decent life, which is interlaced with the love of God and mankind, is the greatest richness and the greatest joy."

IV. SR. ELVIRA SPEAKS

TO THE PARENTS

Sr. Elvira knows well that the family is the beginning of all good, but unfortunately also of all bad. Aside from the work with the youths, she pays great attention to the work with the parents. She wants the parents to take the same spiritual road as the children so that the situation in the family, into which the youths will return after they leave the community, will change. Because, if it does not change, the youths may fall back into the same situation.

"Many youths go back home in the hope that they will find the parents, who are ready to accept them, and are convinced that they have taken the same road as they, themselves, have taken in the communty. This is their right and their deepest need. Very often I witness that they return into the community totally disappointed and this hinders them on their further path.

The healing of the child depends on the healing of the souls and hearts of his parents. Parents, love your children again, believe and search courageously for the gift of faith because without trust in God you cannot regain the trust in your children!

For children it is not enough to have received 'everything', but they want a father, who is worthy, humble and good, who can listen and who is aware that he has to still learn some-thing, even if it were from his own child. The youths want parents, who are decent, honest, worthy, generous and faith-ful. The father and the mother, who are satisified just to have given life to their child and secure the material possibilities for him, which are surely useful, and are only concerned that the child is 'someone' in this world, with a good job and a beautiful house, these parents can hardly regain trust in their child that has disappointed them.

God has invited the parents to give physical life, the greatest gift, so that all other gifts can be received and it would be terrible if they would have said NO to the gift of life! But it is not the parents, who decide for the life of their child! God has decided, together with them, for their child and He creates it in the womb. Even if a child is conceived in violence, in unfaithfulness or under the influence of alcohol, it has the right to be born since, before it became their child, it was God's child. However, you can see yourself that it is not enough to give only physical life. The child should always be reborn for the other in love, faithfulness, sincerity, honesty and the willingness to make sacrifices. The child should be led to God because He gives life, the strength for that life and the desire to resist the destruction of life. The destruction of life is a sin. Many have had physical abortions done, while others have had spiritual abortions.

Abortion is a sin, that does much evil to the hearts of our youths, however, there is no sin that could surpass the boundless mercy of God. Under the weight of sin, that we do not confess and not even want to recognize, under that sin, which oppresses us the most, there is Jesus, who asks or begs that we let Him be resurrected. When we justify ourselves and accuse each other, we lose the joy, we remain sad, disappointed and then the disappointment becomes sin. Jesus invites us to give Him everything because He has already paid for everything, He has already been resurrected and has conquered sin. Really, we have the possibility to be healed if we don't remain in the temptation to hide the sin or we remain in a lie, which kills us. It is possible to be healed, even if the sin returns after we have confessed, and we begin to think that God has not forgiven us. Sin does not insult God, who is boundless mercy, love and light, but it insults us, since it is a fruit of our egoism. The sin is a wound which needs an extended healing. We have to recognize the sin, confess it again and repent.

Everything that you see came out of love, everything is ready for you, so that you can experience joy, happiness and love. I thank all parents, who have come from afar even though their children are not here. These are the parents, who always 'give birth anew' to their child, who will never take drugs again."

THE BLESSING OF THE FOUNDATION STONE IN SALUZZO

"Dear friends of life!

It is good to know that you are only living in the present moment and neither know nor perceive, neither see nor learn what is ahead. Many tell me that I am beginning something that I may possibly not finish. That, however, does not interest me. It is good to know that everything is in the plan of God and I don't want to know anything else. This truth gives me peace, great hope and great trust because God also finishes what He begins. This blessing is possible because you have gone together with us on this road towards a goal, which we don't know. We only know that God is faithful. These are only outwardly signs. We have to emphasize that these buildings, 'the village of peace', are an outward sign of what God has begun. What we see from without is only a pale reality of what happens in our hearts, our souls, in the lives of the youths, in my life, in the life of my colleagues and in the families. We are heirs of the kingdom of God, not of things, not of villages, not of the land! We are the true edifice, that God wants to be built for His honor and our joy because we are immortal. We believe and live for eternity.

No one and nothing will stop us: we always start anew with the last youth, who has entered into the community, and God leads us ahead and teaches us to be happy. I thank you all for your trust in our community and in God.

To you, young people, who have experienced a spiritual renewal and have confessed, I have to say, prior to the blessings of the buildings, that each of you has to be this stone. This morning, each one of us has left his load and his sins on this mountain in the sacrament of confession. The most beautiful, the most lively and eternal works that God accomplished have been created on the poverty and misery of mankind, so that no one can boast about himself. Therefore, we are laying our sins into the foundation of this building. Let us feel present in this stone, which the Bishop, as representative of the entire Church and mankind, is blessing. Let us feel as part of this building, that we do not know yet, which, however, is in the plan of God. From a human point of view, it was tried many times to prevent this building from being constructed, since we had been waiting already eight years for the approval and have only received it in these days.

The Lord permits the realization of His plans when and how He wants it; let us try to do in our will His will because only in His will, will our life be successful and the deeds for the redemption of all people will be achieved."

TO THE WOMEN

On the occasion of 'Day of the Woman', organized by the Italian organization for Women, in the Congress Hall of St. Paul in Turin, Sr. Elvira was invited and spoke very lively:

"I live with 260 drug addicts, who help me come closer to God. They believe in me. . . but who am I? Within me, within us are fragility and sin, but God is also within us. And that is what motivates us in our lives. We believe that this is the certainty that we are not anymore ourselves, but that God is within us. When, deep within us, His love, His courage and His patience take root, then He goes through our being, announces Himself, changes us, saves us, changes the lives and where there is despair, fills it with hope. However, one must have the courage to lose one's life. When a woman only clings to her own life, she is nothing else, she is nothing but an unhappy person, a poor 'old spinster'. On the contrary, the woman is the one, who receives life, she owns a great gift—the love, which should be given and the love which courageously goes forward; the love of the woman is the love that conquers death. To be a woman is a wonderful and endless adventure. The woman is, however, most of all, a spiritual being, her value is not recognized by the 'clothes' she wears, but by the true values God gives her. The resurrection was not completed 2000 years ago, but takes place every time when a thought is born in us about forgiveness, patience or love and only then are hope and life born.

In fact, there are no specialists, who can heal the human heart, only God, who created it, can change it. In the community (of drug addicts) we witness true healings of the hearts of the youths, who had been dead and destroyed. This is accomplished by motherly love, which is open to God, so that in the youths hope and the assurance that God loves them is born again. Through her gifts, the woman is closest to God; but when she turns to death, when she refuses serving life, she becomes her own most dangerous enemy, the most dangerous enemy of the family and the community. A healthy woman, who serves lovingly, is the greatest gift to the community. Be proud to be a woman, give God your heart! You have Mary as a model. Don't be afraid to love completely, do not be afraid to lose your life, because you will find it a hundredfold in your children and in the youths. Stop the deadly work of Eve, the old woman, the woman of sin and offense, the woman, who spoke with the evil one and who executed the deeds, he seduced her to do. Return to the God of life and say, as Mary did, "Here I am Lord," and everything in your life will change. The world today poses a question, as it is posed in the Bible, who will find a strong woman? Happy is the child, who is born from such a mother, happy is her son, who has such a wife and you will be happy to have her as a daughter-in-law. Your family will be peaceful and happy because a strong woman and mother creates the conditions to lead her family back into the earthly paradise, in which love, life and the friendship with God reign; a paradise, in which there are no hiding places and there is no fear, neither from God nor from each other. Serve life and, through Mary, the God of life will be your reward already here and most assuredly in eternity."

FALL IN LOVE WITH JESUS

September 25, 1995

"Dear children! Today I invite you to fall in love with the Most Holy Sacrament of the Altar. Adore Him, little children, in your Parishes and in this way you will be united with the entire world. Jesus will become your friend and you will not talk of Him like someone whom you barely know. Unity with Him will be a joy for you and you will become witnesses to the love of Jesus that He has for every creature. Little children, when you adore Jesus you are also close to me. Thank you for having responded to my call."

"In the message of September, 25, 1995, Our Lady invites us to fall in love with Jesus in the Eucharist. I am convinced that Our Lady is interested in each one of us because we are all Her sons. What does it mean to fall in love? Can one fall in love when one runs away from the beloved person, can one fall in love if one never looks into one another's eyes, can one fall in love if one does not listen with the heart to the beloved person? One cannot fall in love if one does not learn to be in silence, in the silence of thoughts, of the heart, of the eyes, of the soul, in the silence between us. One cannot fall in love if one does not remain with the other. This is why we have perpetual adoration in the community. This is surely the wish of Our Lady and Jesus. Jesus wants us to get to know Him. The adoration of Jesus connects us, as our Lady says, with the whole world. Our Lady says that, in this way, Jesus will become a friend, whom we will know. For us, this means that we will not talk about Him as we would talk about someone, whom we hardly know. Being together with Jesus and one another will be the source of our joy. So you will become the one, who will be able to help the other to meet Jesus, who gave His love for that brother, who had known nothing about Jesus.

Jesus sends His disciples into the world by twos. This is a rule in our community, by twos, so that there is always togetherness. Jesus also says that He is there, where two pray together. This means that the person next to you gives you an assurance of the presence of Christ. Thus, when you go by twos, Jesus is with you in a special way.

But not only Jesus, also Our Lady is with us. She says, when we adore Jesus, She is also with us. She is always in adoration with Jesus. Before we begin to be with Jesus in adoration, Our Lady is already there. She is already adoring. Our guardian angel is also with us. He also sees the face of Christ and adores Him. You see, we are not alone.

Our Lady came to Medjugorje and reminds us of the truths we already know. In the first message, She says, "I came to tell you that God exists." You see, your parents knew that God exists, but that is not enough, they did not pray with you, they did not talk enough with you, they did not give birth to you

spiritually the way Jesus wanted. Thus conflicts and divorces arose; therefore, they did not have time for you. I am not judging them, they did not know any better.

But we are in Her school. And Mary wants that our knowledge becomes love and even more, to fall in love. When She told us that God exists, then She said, "God loves you." Now She asks of us that we fall in love with Christ and, in order to fall in love, one has to remain. When we remain, we must first purify our heart, our soul and our mind of empty thoughts.

In our life, those persons who have loved us, those persons, who did acts of love, mercy, forgiveness and patience for us, have left traces and not those, who talked much and persuaded us to do something.

We have the need to be loved. Love is what changes life and develops trust. Because, only when we feel that someone loves us, is it possible for us to trust him.

We must go with Jesus into silence, into adoration, allow Jesus to love us so that His love comes into our hearts and into the depths of our souls and does not remain somewhere outside of us, outside of our soul. Sometimes we try to think up beautiful prayers and tell them to Our Lord. The Lord does not expect that from us. He knows everything we want to say to Him. Now we must start to answer with our heart.

One also must know that true love very often originates from pain and suffering. To love, therefore, means to suffer. We learn to adore Jesus in the Eucharist. When we are before Him, He will speak to us. He is the only source of love that the Father has announced to us. Our Lady knows that and this is why She says we should fall in love with the Eucharist. If this falling in love does not happen, your heart will be dry, cold and abandoned.

Sometimes it is a problem for us to accept love. That must be learned. This is why we have to go to Jesus.

We should follow this rule: **DURING THE DAY WE WORK, AND DURING THE NIGHT WE PRAY!**

I was recently in Brazil. The Bishop, who received us, is a man of prayer. He gets up at four in the morning and prays. A few days before the message of Sept. 25th, he asked us to go into adoration; but he asked this not only of us, but of the entire diocese. When I heard the message, I read it to him over the telephone. He was overjoyed like a small child. Many listened to him and so did we. However, one must have the courage to suggest something like that.

During adoration, a change occurs in the soul and that is why changes begin in the family and in the relationships within the family, togetherness develops and so a dialogue becomes possible. The children find the right time and the right place to talk with their parents. Naturally, it is necessary that the parents fall in love with the Eucharist and that they can also remain in front of Jesus in silence. Even if it is only fifteen minutes in the beginning, things will change. Do you remember the song which says 'where you pass by, life begins?'

We are here to renew life. Yesterday a young man told me, "Sister, not only my physical life is being renewed, I also feel inwardly renewed, my thoughts and my feelings are different, I am free to talk about my life. I have realized that, when I am afraid to talk about my fall, about my addiction, then I become even more enslaved. I am no longer lost and depressed, the Lord has renewed me!"

It is always wonderful to hear such testimonies. He also told me, "My internal renewal continues. I free myself more and more from my fears, I am no longer afraid of people, I think completely different, my soul is new!"

Healing begins with the healing of the thoughts, with changes in thinking, then with the healing of the soul, the feelings and the heart. One must continuously work on this.

In Brazil, I was in a community, directed by Father Sometti, in which there are about 100 small children. Every morning they get up at 5:45 and celebrate the Eucharist together. Mass lasts one and a half hours because they sing much and during the night they get up and go into adoration. In this community, which has only existed for nine months, I found children from nine months to 16 years of age. They pray, as we do here. Wonderful! Also the smallest children get up for adoration. A young boy asked, " Why are you waking me up?" The answer was clear: "We will adore Jesus so that He is not alone!"

For all this, one only needs determination.

I saw so many happy faces. One must not wait for heaven in order to see paradise. Paradise exists already on earth when you meet clear, open and shiny eyes and a clean heart, which is free of any slavery, free of any haste and not bound to any pattern. Such a heart is already filled with paradise.

These children are waiting for you. I ask myself how you could go there if you have not already fallen in love with the Eucharist and because you don't yet like to go into adoration. Once when I went into adoration there, there was a family with four children already present, the youngest of which was four years old and the eldest nine. They were all kneeling. It was wonderful to see that.

One day the community prepared a meeting for all children; there are many of them on the streets, and no one takes care of them. Father Giuseppe Sometti searches for them and brings them into the community. This was a true feast of life, a true Eucharist. The heart is being renewed here.

You, who want to go to Brazil, must first ask Our Lady that you fall in love with the Eucharist. That is the only condition.

Today I can say that many cannot rear children because they do not go into adoration. Many mothers cannot pray, they do not adore, they are still more physical, flesh and blood, than spiritual. Such mothers can only rear nervous, frightened, anxious and confused children. We must become spiritual mothers. It is easiest to give the child physical life, but one must not leave it at that. The mother must continue to give birth to the child through her sacrifice, her prayer and her renunciation. The child will grow. It is dangerous to worry too much about the body and to neglect the heart and the soul.

In this community of small children, I saw that God really fills up human beings. The children don't have a physical mother, however, what is given to them through prayer and adoration, through love and sacrifice makes them happy. We will also go there, in order to help this community, but we must become like children, as Jesus says."

FINDING EXPRESSIONS OF
LOVE AGAIN AND AGAIN

"Spiritual and physical life grow together, develop together and mature together.

Love grows in self-discipline. Why are we afraid? Because we think that the one who criticizes us does not love us. We must realize that we come from situations, which have destroyed us and that we, therefore, cannot love. But we will learn it. This is the daily work. One must endure; love is enkindled in the heart. Pray for the one, to whom you must say something. Love is born in prayer! Learn to see those, who love you, and try to find in others what is good; learn to accept the wonderful works, which God achieves in our brothers. When you see, that someone is not growing, pray for him, wait a certain amount of time, then approach him with love, and say to him, "What you are doing is not good, it hinders you on your way, you are wasting the time that is given to you. Later you will not have it." The one, who does not love, has no right to reproach the other, even if he has lived 10 years in the community. The one, whose heart is cold, sad and proud, should keep silent and adore Jesus day and night and ask for a healing. Because, if your heart is still so when you come out of adoration, you will destroy yourself again, as well as the others. Love means to suffer. First, suffer with love and then try to criticize your brother. Give up coffee, get up during the night for half an hour and in secret, without anyone seeing you, clean the shoes or wash the socks of your brother, whom you do not love. When you begin to love, love will motivate you to do small works that bring joy and peace. The inventiveness of love knows no bounds. Let us decide together today that we will live love and will try to find again and again expressions of love, beginning with a glance and smile. One should transform pain and suffering into love. We shall ask the Lord today to teach us expressions of love. If you see that someone leaves his belongings somewhere, where he should not leave them, you should put them back in their place and tell him about it later. Love is not a feeling, but a life of concrete steps and deeds."

THE TRUTH WILL SET YOU FREE

"The Lord gives you the grace to hear His word. Today He speaks much to you, to the addicts here and to all other addicts and the youths on the street. You, however, hear His word about freedom. But, if you bury His word within you, not knowing what you have received, then you are unfair to those, who do not hear the word of God. They are waiting for it, they are thirsty for the same word. You must announce it to them, but when this word of God remains in the chapel here, you are not honest and you are not doing your duty. Man is invited to live in peace and in joy and for you this joy begins today; and those are wrong, who believe that joy comes from something else. Neither the husband, nor the wife, nor the children, nor money can give this joy. A wise wife once wrote to me, "I have realized that my children, although they are wonderful and good, and motivate me to be good and to change, do not completely fill me with joy." I must say, if a child does not motivate one to be good, then it is really abnormal and a monster. This is why God gave us the community in this time so that we all, the parents as well as the children, change each other. I see that wonderful things happen in those communities where there are children. Thoughts are being purified and cleansed. Persons, who do not give up pleasures, not only sexual, but also culinary ones, or the enjoyments that come from pride; persons, who rejoice in victories by humiliating others, who rejoice in being right, who think they are better than the others, those persons make themselves and others unhappy. There actually are persons, who have degraded themselves to the pleasures on the animal level.

If you believe that material things will make you happy, it is a sign that you are not yet a mature person, that you are not yet perfect, that you are still on this animal level. Imagine how a poor girl feels, who lives with someone who only knows sexual enjoyment. This is complete poverty, misery; it is not worthy of human beings. It is sad when a person does not have the strength to resist these enticements of pleasure and uses the others for his egotistical urges. To chase after pleasures dehumanizes man.

That is why we first have to recognize our personal dimension. We must realize that we are persons, who can love and suffer for others, who recognize their values and who do not forget that in each one of us, there is a hidden possibility to live these values. A person, who cannot love, is not even worthy to look into the face of another person; for example, someone, who cannot love, will not be able to resist the temptation to masturbate and, because of that, he will lose the joy and, with his sadness and unrest, he will burden the community. The problem is within you because you are humiliated, because you have not prepared yourself for this fight against these temptations. The temptations will always come, but you must not satisfy them because you cannot live if you are dependent on the pleasures of the moment. We must prepare ourselves for the fight against these pleasures, the fight against pornography. You know that the pleasures, that you ran after, have destroyed your heart and soul, they did not make you happy. I must point out that all this has not destroyed you, thank God, because Jesus Christ, the Resurrected, is within you. He wins, in spite of our sin, our weakness, our wounds. That is our joy, that is our peace. So someone is within us, who can conquer all evil and all bad habits. It is as if we were in a bottomless pit and see the blue sky and feel the freedom from afar. But on this road to inner freedom and one's own heaven, lie temptations. One must conquer them.

Each one of us found himself in his own tunnel, we have all tried it, each in his own fashion. You teach me and show me, who is really an addict. You are my teachers. I shall not go to school, not to the psychologist, psychiatrist or doctor. They talk and talk. You are my school. During these 12 years of school with you, I believe I have learned something. And yesterday I understood something new. It also happened to me-that I started to believe that I am someone and something special. This is my tunnel. I know that the word of God tells us that the proud will be burned like hay. When? In the hour of our death? No. Already now all proud and self-centered are burning like hay. Each time when we crave for pleasures, we are hopelessly in the tunnel. There are persons, who do not want to move and so they remain in the hell of hopelessness and they scream, condemn, swear, get drunk, they live in hatred and distrust. This can last forever. We must decide for ourselves. We do not want to remain in the tunnel because our sins are in the tunnel and they are our tunnel.

Even if we believe there is no hope for us, someone told us, "Let me be resurrected. I died and I want to be resurrected so that you will be liberated from your sin. You have the right to come out of your evil." This is the possibility, which is always offered us. We must be courageous and must not remain in our sins. We must make an act of will and try. I do not want to think or believe that I am better than others, but I want to try to do what makes me happy: to be humble, good, and generous, accept the brother, speak with him, forgive, be merciful; I want to become like Jesus. This is not a theory. There are persons, who have so befriended Jesus that they have become like Him. I want to live for others the love, the mercy, the forgiveness and the goodness of Jesus. Why do I want to repeat this? Because this is the greatest joy in life. There is nothing that gives more fullness to life than the friendship of Jesus. This is no theory because goodness, mercy, forgiving, purity are not empty and nebulous words, as far as their meaning is concerned. They are clear and concrete. When I accept Jesus, there is resurrection and the victory over death. God became man and He says to us that we are His children, that He does everything for us and we are precious to Him. Jesus tells everyone, "Whatever you ask my Father in my name, it will be given to you." In each situation, also when we are upsetting each other, humiliating each other, using and misusing each other, He is always telling us, "I love you, I like you, I want to save you."

If we want to be filled with the Holy Spirit, we have a model how to live joy and peace, love and generosity, how to give one's life for another: **THE EUCHARIST**. That is why it is necessary to look directly at the Eucharist and then He will show us His heart through the power of prayer.

In prayer you will realize who you are and what you can do, where you are and who can help you. I tell you this because I also fall daily and because I am a witness of your falls and rises. Above my sin, my ignorance, my desire for pleasure, my pride and my self-centredness, my craving for honor, my brutality, my self-conduct, above all this and behind all this, there is always one who says, "I want to save you, I came to liberate you from your heavy chains. Le me be resurrected in you, allow me to do so and I will destroy all your sins." He wants to do this, He wants to do this with us today. We must not give room to anger, mistrust, bitterness and non-forgiving from which Jesus liberates us. One must believe in a person, even if he is the greatest sinner, like myself. However, I must say that I want to be resurrected in the Lord because He will give life to this dry heart and to those thoughts, which attack and give no peace, and He will calm our fantasies. We know that Jesus wants to liberate us from this difficult life in sin, for example, if someone does not live in truth. We must learn to live in truth and must not allow large and small lies to take hold of us. The one, who does not live in truth, can have no joy. Jesus said, "that the truth will liberate you." The truth will liberate us from our sin and we will be good persons and not only 'appear' as such. New people! The future lies in your being good, the future of society and the Church. The Pope always says to the youth, "You young people, you are the hope of the world, the future is in your hands, you must be free." There are many, who follow him.

To be free does not mean to sin no more, but to admit our sins freely. We do not remain in sin, we believe in the resurrection. This does not mean that I want you all to become priests. No! I would like for you to become persons like God wants you to be. If you do not become such persons, you will not be happy. No person is happy in sin. Sin humiliates the person and that is why the Lord does not want you to be in such a situation.

He does not want you to be bound by the chains of sin, He wants you to be free. We must be witnesses, who announce the future not only with words but with our life. Each one of you has received a precious treasure when he entered into the community. You must be witnesses with your life. One should be a witness for the Resurrected Christ. He was resurrected and He also wants to be resurrected in you today."

THE RENEWAL OF THE
SACRAMENT OF MARRIAGE

It is a fact that many youths, who entered into the community, have left behind a wife and children at home. As they are being healed from their addiction, attain their inner freedom, come out of the tunnel of self-centredness and pride, they renew their relationship towards themselves, the family, nature and God. The process of this renewal includes especially the wife and the children, who have been deeply wounded by the husband and father. When the community finds that someone is ready for the renewal of the sacrament of marriage, then this is celebrated in a festive manner. A true healing takes place at the root.

Sister Elvira talked about one such festive occasion:

"More and more often we encounter marriages that were entered into without a mature decision, without the clear realization of what was happening and what one had decided for, without the maturity of selfless mutual love. This is why more and more marriages break up, not only those of drug addicts, but in general. A young man told me, "Before I went to confession and before I was married, I took drugs. My best man was a 'type', who had sold me heroin. I was totally absent. Now I am slowly realizing everything and I see the terrible results in my life and in the life of my wife. She has remained faithful to me and has reared our child, whom we conceived in the state of addiction. When I heard that we can renew our marriage vows in a festive manner in the community, I was filled with joy!"

Joy fills you now because you realize what you are doing, because you are alive and you realize that you can serve in life. What you are living through at the moment, while renewing your sacrament of marriage, is a good sign. A decision is being healed, which you had made at a time when you were not mature enough for it. This renewal of the sacrament says yes to your new awareness, gives new life, makes the tree blossom anew, which had so many dry branches: the indifference, unawareness, sensual interests, fears, the search for the fastest way to attain wealth and all other dry branches of evil, that kill family relations. The only true foundation of the family is Jesus Christ.

I am convinced that you and all youths within the community will live marriage consciously, by accepting the gift of the new life with responsibility, and when you say in front of Christ, 'I choose you as my partner for my entire life,' that this will also be done in faithfulness and love."

When Sister Elvira prepares the youths for marriage, she always talks about four pillars, on which one builds the common future of the family.

1. **HUMILITY** - That means to have the strength to say to the other person, "I need you!"

How much sorrow must you endure until you are able to admit that you need him?!

2. **SACRIFICE** - If you don't realize that you have to sacrifice something in order to show the other your love, you will not be able to love. There is no love without pain and the

love, which is not ready to sacrifice itself, to sacrifice something within itself even itself, is no love, but exploitation, selfishness and abuse.

3. **THE SMILE** - It seems so small, but it is very successful. When you are humble, you will not be a person, who holds grudges, you will not retaliate evil with evil and you will not have the need to always be right.

When you are humble, you forgive easily, you forget, you begin anew, you trust and you have the strength to smile. When you don't have the strength to smile, it means that you cannot forget, that you are not emptying your heart of bad feelings and that peace cannot dwell within your heart.

4. **THE PRAYER** - This is the most important means in a union of two souls and two hearts.

When a couple does not pray, they will not have the strength to remain in truth and the lie, dishonesty, the masks, the superficiality, the escape and unfaithfulness will begin. In order for the couple to remain together, they must both have the strength to spend some moments together on their knees.

V. I WILL GET UP AND WALK

One of the most difficult problems in the healing process is precisely the entry into the community. The addicts do not want to enter into the community as long as they have the hope to find a small piece of bread, that they can somehow buy with the money they need for their 'fix'. In this process, however, the parents must perform the most difficult task. Sister Elvira suggests an action, which is very bitter for the hearts of the mother and father: "Throw him out of the house so he will not be able to exploit you any longer!" The parents are always afraid that something worse will happen. As long as the parents do not have the courage to throw their drug addicted child out of the house, usually the decision for healing cannot develop.

When a young man or girl make the decision to be healed, they come to one of the communities, which welcome them into a so-called colloquium, a meeting.

In Croatia, these meetings take place in Tugari, near Split. Each Tuesday the addict has to appear there alone or with his parents. In these meetings, it will be decided if he really wants to enter into the community. Between these colloquiums, it is possible to come into the community during the day, to live there, but in the evening, he has to look for his own sleeping accommodation.

This goes on until the day when the community is convinced that the addict is ready to enter into the community and to accept its rules. This can also last several weeks.

On one hand, the community is always ready to accept a youth unconditionally, on the other hand, the colloquiums make his previous contact with the community necessary before the permission for his entry is given. The community is not concerned whether the young addict takes drugs during this time. This seems to be a contradiction.

But the community has to protect itself. For those, who are already in the community, it is from a psychological point of view always good when someone new comes into the community. However, if the youths are let into the community too quickly, there is a danger that they will leave the community again; but each departure puts a strain on those, who live in the community and brings back memories of the past and creates problems, with which they have to deal again.

From the moment the addict enters into the community, it takes on the complete care for him. Neither the parents nor any other institution has the 'right' to do anything. Everything is put under the control of the organization of the community. During the first eight months, no contact whatsoever is allowed with the parents, friends or another person from the outside so that the addict can 'stand on his own feet'. Later there is the possibility, and it is being used, to spend several days or weeks within the families or surroundings, in which they had lived, as a so-called 'trial' and return back into the community.

In the community of Sister Elvira, no medication, no psychologists and no psychiatrists are allowed to treat the withdrawal symptoms.

Once I asked her what is being done with those who have the so-called withdrawal symptoms. The answer was clear: No one has died of these symptoms, one dies from the overdoses. In such cases, they remain in the community and help each other.

The whole process, from the beginning of the actual addiction to the healing within the community, takes place from the deadly illness, that the drugs make even stronger, up to the moment when one begins to love life.

Let those speak, who have, in one way or another, gone on this road from their death sentence through drugs to living the resurrection. This is why I bring here the testimonies of young people, who are living in the community at the time that this book is being written. There are also the testimonies of those, who have finished their path in the community and have returned into the world and are continuing their lives there. It is also very important to hear the testimonies of their parents.

Each testimony is a story in itself, sad and full of pain, shocking and dramatic, but still full of hope and joy for life.

No one can enjoy life as much
as the one, who has experienced death.
No one can enjoy togetherness as much
as the one, who has experienced loneliness.
No one experiences freedom as intensely
as the one, who has lost it and was enslaved.

No one can honor the family as much
as the one, who has deceived each family rule.
No one can pray as much as the one,
who has thrown away every contact with God.
No one can help as gratefully as the one,
who does not forget that someone has helped him.
Because there, where sin was in surplus,
the graces were given also in greater abundance.

So I give you these testimonies with much love and care, as if I would put into your hands a fragile flower, which was wounded by the disregard of those passing by.

I give you these testimonies, which are a sign of love to the reader and listener, as if I would give you a wounded pearl, in which its woundedness becomes even more beautiful.

I would like you to read them with love and listen to them with your heart. Open your heart, let it sympathize, let it be touched by the 'fall' and, even more, let it be happy over the successes, let it cry over the dead and be happy with the re-surrected, so that the love for life can grow within your heart and that the courage to protect and respect each life can develop from that love.

(The testimonies in this book are given as they were told!)

1. KENNY ALSTON

It was a very long road from my house of birth in Georgia to Medjugorje. There was much joy, sorrow, pain and sad-ness. I lived in darkness for 23 years. I lived with drugs and alcohol and thought this was the true life in liberty and inde-pendence. Today I live in the community 'Cenacolo' and have learned that the freedom and independence, which I thought I had, were only a deception. The deception was a mask, be-hind which I could take drugs and alcohol. Behind this mask, I even thought that what I did was good, because I did what the world expected of me.

My life began at the moment when my family left me and this was when I was 14 months old. I was born in Atlanta, Georgia, in the USA. My family left me and handed me over to a family in west-Georgia and they adopted me. The reason why my family left me was very simple. My mother could not care for us any longer. My new family was related to my mother. The same family adopted two of my brothers and sisters. Later they returned to our mother, but I did not want this. I don't remember well but I know that they told me that I was very sick when I was small. I have to admit that they loved me and that they helped me spiritually. They had time for me and I know that they sacrificed much for me. I grew up on a farm and it was not an easy life. The father of this family was an alcoholic, although he was a Baptist. Because of financial difficulties, the family lost the farm. Later the father found a job in a construction company.

The mother of this family worked very hard, she was often at home, she worked in the parish and also visited the sick. I must say that both father and mother were good models for me.

They told me that it was important to go to church and to be a good person. I emphasize this because I do not want to accuse them for my using drugs, this was my decision. They reared me as best as they could, but I saw life differently. I had problems in speaking, I stuttered, I was very shy, but I was also bigger and stronger than all the other kids. My new parents were often asked, who this young boy was, who was so different from the other children. The mother always watched over me, she always tried to have me near her and to keep me occupied. So that happened what usually happens in black families—the mother cares more for the children and the father works continuously and is absent from the family.

Now I know the reason why I started to take drugs was the missing presence of my father in my life.

Now I also know that the problem of black families and the discrimination in America at that time were also reasons for my drugs. There were separate schools, buses and hospitals for us.

Now I see that I wanted to free myself from this. I began with sports, especially basketball. In basketball, I was very successful and this helped me to finish high school on time. Then I began to dress better and to travel. I became even a better basketball player and, at the same time, spent more money and began to drink. My family was proud of me, many admired me, but no one could imagine how I felt inside.

During this time, many high schools and universities wanted to recruit me. I decided for the University of South Georgia. They promised me everything because I was such I good basketball player.

When I got a place at the University, I thought that the door for a very interesting life had been opened for me. I thought I was finally free. My freedom consisted of spending entire nights in bars, not going home and searching for women. At the same time, I practiced basketball a lot. I was one of the few blacks at the University and this began to bother me again and I felt lost. A student suggested I take drugs to solve my problems, to run quicker, to play basketball even more successfully, to study better and get along better with the whites. He convinced me and I began to take hashish, then cocaine, then LSD and finally heroin. I no longer studied and drugs and alcohol became important in my life. In spite of this, I still played basketball well. Many admired me as a superstar with a good car and beautiful suits. The newspapers also wrote about me. But my reality was already sad—I became a drug addict, I did not finish class and, for one season, I did not get permission to play basketball. In the meantime, my girlfriend became pregnant and my daughter was born. I left them both. I could not care for them.

I went back home to my biological family. My mother was very closed towards me. She reproached me constantly.

(Again there was no real conversation as it should be in every family. The parents should not hide anything from their children and have no secrets from them. This wounds the relationships in the family and particularly causes instability of feelings.)

I returned to school and completed it. Professional teams were interested in me and I decided to join the 'Philadelphia

76'ers' for two years. I thought neither of my daughter nor of my family. I began to live badly again. This cost me my career. I returned back home and began to sell cars and drugs. During the day, I worked on my first job and at night, on the second. Again, I broke all ties with my family. The police began to look for me. My girlfriend asked for money for the child. This was a legal order. I began to visit my daughter once a month. This also did not last long because I fell deeper and deeper into living badly. I sold cocaine.

So I finally wore many masks on my face: one at home, a second in front of my daugther, the third, in front of people I sold cars to and the fourth in front of those, to whom I sold drugs. My life became more and more difficult and unbearable.

Again I tried to play basketball. In college I became a basketball referee. I earned a lot of money, but this money only dragged me into more drugs. I continued to sell drugs although I had enough money. I tried all types of drugs.

I decided to marry. My wife was a teacher. Many thought that I was again successful in life and envied me. But I fell deeper and deeper, began to stay away from work, to falsify cheques and to make debts. Finally I lost my job. These changes in my work and in sports, this winning and losing lasted almost 10 years. Finally I divorced my wife. It was a complete break from all friends and family.

Then I began to look for help in different institutions for drug addicts. But nothing helped. I changed places, towns, friends and communities. I was also in the hospital, I went to psychiatrists and psychologists but this also did not help. In the meantime I got married again and divorced again.

All this happened during the time from 1973 to 1994, almost an entire 22 years, full of pain, sorrow, success, falls and attempts to get up again and new experiences of weaknesses. I also was in jail. Several times I was near death.

In June, 1994, after having lived on the streets of St. Augustine, Florida, I went into a community which helps the homeless. This was the hardest day in my life: completely on the floor, disillusioned, without any hope or strength to try anything. I was sick of everything. I asked the responsible person in the community to give me money for the bus so that I could leave town. I only wanted to run away.

When I left, I heard a voice in my heart that said, "Why don't you ask these people if a community exists that can help you to free yourself from the drugs? Don't be afraid, I can do this!"

I went back and inquired about such a community. They told me that they could help me.

When I now think back, I think about the words of Jesus, "Seek and you will find!" This was Monday, the 20th of June, 1994. They called a community in St. Augustine, Florida. It was the community of Sister Elvira, 'Our Lady of Hope'. This was my entry into a new life.

When I met the young guys in the community for the first time, they all were happy and cheerful, they prayed and worked. They talked about Our Lady, St. Joseph and the saints. They all appeared to be crazy to me. My first impression was: This place is not for me! Since I was a Baptist, I knew nothing about Our Lady or the saints. Aside from the thought that these guys were all crazy, I also was jealous because I knew that this was exactly what I had been looking for during my wandering around.

In this community, I learned that joy comes from prayer. Now I don't need any drugs because I pray. Today, prayer means much to me. I can also listen to my conscience. When I was an addict, I did everything to dull my conscience. I did not want to listen to it. For me, prayer was a medicine, it healed me. I admit that I have changed in my heart, as well as in my soul. And I still try to change daily.

In this community, prayer is in the first place. Sister Elvira often says, "When we pray, everything else will be given to us." She tells us that one should pray, even if one does not believe. What happens here, is the school of life. Who enters, decides for life. I have learned to keep my dignity, to respect others and to behave well. I have learned to be obedient, to help the others, to live with the others, to serve the others and ask for nothing in return. I have learned to be humble. Now I realize that my pride has hindered me to accept the reality that Jesus is the answer and that He waits for me with extended arms on the cross. I have realized that Jesus lived, died and was resurrected and that He lives among us. I feel Him so vividly in our community. Jesus accepts us, as we are, and gives us everything we need. But in order to do that, He needs the others. This is our community here.

There must be sacrifices and the fight for inner freedom from any addiction. I must admit there are still many things I do not undertand. It is not always easy, there also came temptations to leave the community. But I have decided and so I repeat every day, "I want to remain here!"

Today I have a beautiful relationship with my family. In September 1996, after 10 years, I was able to visit my daughter.

Today, people often ask me what miracle happened in my life. I have no supernatural, mystical experiences, but today I am able to love the others, which I was not able to do before. That is most important for me.

In October 1996, I became a Catholic, I went to Confession for the first time and received Holy Communion. This is a great experience for me because I now can receive Jesus.

Now I see that God had really not left me through all this time. I left Him. It was very difficult for me to accept the fact that God did not leave me or judge me. Now I realize how great His love is and that one cannot serve two masters and that one cannot live with one leg in the light and with the other in the darkness. This whole time the drug was my god for whom I sacrificed everything.

In this community I got to know the power of prayer, which has led me out of darkness. In short, I can say, my way led me from the darkness into the light, for which I am very grateful to God.

2. STEFANO ARAGNO

(He was not an addict, but he came into the community because he wanted to help for a certain period of time. He now studies Theology and wants to become a priest.)

I want to tell you something about my life, about what happened to me and especially I want to thank God for the gift of the community, for the gift of life. I have been living in the community for over six years and for me, it was a great gift from God that I got to know it. I did not enter into the community because of drug problems, but rather because I did not want to go into the army. So I chose the possibility to work in social services. I served my time, but I enjoyed it and felt the wish to continue living in the communty. When I entered to become a member of this family, I thought that I was the one, who had to help the others; I was convinced that I was a decent person because I came from a Christian family and I thought I was ok. In school I did well, no one had problems with me and I lived my life, but I had no joy. But when I met the young men in the community, who had totally gone astray during life, I felt my own failures and realized and had to admit that I was exaclty like them, with the same fears, just as lost as they were, with the same masks on the face, with the same sadness in my heart. So I decided to continue my life with them, to share joy and sadness, happiness and unhappiness with them. In thanking God and His grace, I can say today I am content and full of enthusiasm for everything that life offers me from day to day. What I feel and what I want to say is that life is a gift and a seed with unbelievable possibilities for development and growth. I feel much energy within me, a great desire, an unbelievable will for life because life is a precious gift and life is an eternal value, it never ceases, life conquers death. I see in the community the resurrection of many young guys, whom I know, and I have learned that the community gives me an opportunity to get to know the concrete faith, the true faith, that throws me on my knees, the faith, which does not allow to only search for my pleasures. This is the faith I have always searched for, even when I argued with my parents, who I thought were hypocrites. Today I feel that the faith, which the community shows me and which is being lived in the community, is actually the true faith, a faith, that does not let you rest, the faith, which enkindles you, the concrete faith, that flows through your fingers and always leaves joy behind. With the help of the community, I discovered so many things within me, which are very important to me, but especially the beauty of life, about which I always dreamt about, which I always wanted and had, but never valued.

I began to value the gift of life when I saw so many young guys around me, who had lost it and were searching for it tirelessly. I saw that their fall was also my fall and in their loneliness, I recognized my own loneliness. In the drama of their senseless life, I discovered the drama of the senselessness of my own life, even though many thought that I was doing well. What I want to say to you is that with God, life is not lost, even when—from a human point of view—it looks completely destroyed.

3. MARCO ZAPPELLA

I am Marco. I was born in Bergamo, Italy. I was born in a Christian family.

I have an older brother and sister. Today I live in the community of Sister Elvira. I have been here already for six years. I am very content that I am in the community and that I am alive. Before coming into the community, I used heroin for six years. Today I realize that there are many reasons for my using heroin. I suddenly began taking it, for example, when I was angry at someone or another similar reason. I did not begin to use drugs just like that, it happened suddenly. Now I know that the root for the drug lies deeper than the first injection. The drugs began much, much earlier for me. That is why I want to talk about my family and my life in the family before I start talking about the drugs. In this way, I think we will better understand my reasons for taking drugs.

I must admit that I was also happy because my family always wanted me to be well. I admit that I grew up in a Christian family that went to Church at least on Sundays. I know that is not enough to be a good Christian. But I soon grew tired of all these things. I was also an altar boy and knew many priests, but somehow I got tired of it all. I also remember many moments in my family when we were nervous and uptight. We prayed little. I remember that my father went to Mass alone at a certain time and my mother went alone at another time. When I saw that they did not go together, I did not realize that it is important to do things together with them. I saw these things already when I was six years old. My father had time for everything, for work, for recreation, for friends, but for me, he never had time. Today I know my father had to pay back many debts, that he had to work much, but today I also know that he could have easily given five minutes for us children. I love my father, but those five minutes I did not receive from him, still torture me. These are small things but I see that they wounded the trust I had for my father and my mother. I want to talk about a small incident because it is important to be able to understand me.

After I had smoked a cigarette for the first time, I returned home and my clothes smelled from the smoke. My mother noticed this immediately and asked me if I had smoked. I decisively said no. She asked me again. I said again that I had not smoked and that I had been in a bar with my friends and that they had all smoked there and that is why my clothes smelled. My mother accepted this answer. But what I had said was not the truth. I remember that I had wanted to tell the truth, really wanted to say it, but no one demanded this of me, they didn't care. A cigarette is nothing. Today, many young people do it, they try a cigarette and then a little more. When there is no truth in the family, everything turns up side down. Later on everything is permitted. At the beginning, it is always small things. This happened when I was 14 years old.

When I was 15, I did not listen either to my mother or father. I worked at what I wanted. They wanted me to study; I also wanted that, but I also wanted money, to be free and independent. I remember, that I always wanted to be better than the others, more skilled than the others. I looked for the company of older guys. But I did not feel comfortable with them. But I needed this, I wanted to feel bigger.

From there, it was only a short road to marijuana and from there one easily drifts into heavier drugs. When I began to take heroin, I did not think I was a drug addict. As long as I did not use an injection, I thought that the others were the drug addicts, and not I. I believed that I was smarter than the others, that I got along better than they, that I was more intelligent and that I could stop when I wanted to. This was a deception. Not only heroin, but also joints! But even then I did not understand how people destroy themselves. When I began to use injections, I was afraid. In these moments, I found a strange comfort. I always saw guys in worse situations than myself and comforted myself that I was not really like they were. I was never in prison, I had no reason to steal and I had no need to sell drugs. But soon, I also had to begin to sell drugs and to steal. My fall happened quickly. I destroyed myself completely. I only weighed 50 kilos when I came into the community. I had no will to do anything, no strength for any work. The only desire, that had remained, was to take drugs. I spent up to $500 a day. The more drugs there were, the more often I took them daily. I lost all dignity, I started to forget everything, I was dishonest and untrue with everyone.

I took advantage of the feelings of my parents only for my own benefit and for drugs.

Today I am especially thankful for two days in my life and I bless them. The first day was when my parents had the strength to say to me, "Either you decide to go into the community and we will help you or you leave this house!" On this day I was really scared. I understood that I could not continue like that. I had no intention to stop taking drugs; but I was afraid to continue with this habit. The second day, that I bless and for which I am thankful, was when I met Sister Elvira. When our eyes met, hope began to grow within me. When I entered into the community, I remember it as if it were yesterday, I got out of the car with a cigarette in my mouth. A guy shouted at me from afar that one cannot smoke here. Immediately I said to myself that this community was not for me. I got back into the car again, in which my sister was waiting for me. In the meantime, that guy came up to me and started talking to me. I saw that this guy meant well. I could not understand that because we had only seen each other for the first time. He put his hand on my shoulder and accompanied me into the community. While going to the community, I saw guys, who worked, sang and all appeared happy at work, even though there was much work. To me it seemed impossible that these guys could look so happy, although they had been drug addicts like myself. The desire for a new life arose in me. A good seed fell into my heart. But, after the first day in the community when I arrived home in the evening, the drug conquered me again. It took me three months before I entered into the community. The guys accepted me. It was in the afternoon. On the first day, I went back and forth. What shocked me was that in the evening we went into the chapel. The guys sang and, while they were singing, everything looked beautiful. Then they began to pray the rosary. I did not know what that meant. They began to pray the Hail Mary, one after the other, then ten, then again ten. In my head, thoughts and questions began to spin: What did I get into? These are not drug addicts! This is a mental institution! They are not like myself. I wanted to leave right away. But the guy was with me, whom we call 'the guardian angel'. He was with me at every moment. When we went to sleep, he was with me, when I went to the toilet, he waited for me, when we worked, he was with me, at night when I was in crisis because of the lack of drugs, and I was hot and cold, he was near me. This is the 'guardian angel'. I am sure if no one had been next to me, I would have never been able to free myself from drugs. I must say, thank God, that I found this one in the community 'Cenacolo'.

I found a warm embrace in this community, the embrace of the family, the mother . . .

Today I can say in faith, that in the community I have found the embrace of God, the Father, who is the Father of us all. This is why I not only feel alive but even more, I feel resurrected! I feel reborn. I feel life within me.

When one has spent a certain time in the community, the guardian angel does not follow you as he did during the first days. Slowly trust develops and little by little the community entrusts you with small things, tasks and other people.

Outside of the community, I had lived in such a manner that I had destroyed myself. I had grown physically but spiritually, I had lived only for the drug. I felt that I had remained child-like. The first proof of trust the community gives you are the true great experiences and achievements. It is beautiful to be able to do things on your own and these are the first real joys in the community. Here one learns to live and, after a few months, you, yourself, become a 'guardian angel' for another and this is beautiful. You become a 'guardian angel' for another guy, who had been destroyed by the drug like you, who has problems like you, who cannot sleep at night, like you did not sleep, who during the day, talks every two mintues about drugs, exactly like you, who wants to leave and you must convince him to stay; you must remain with him. During this time, I have been a 'guardian angel' several times. It is hard work, but very beautiful. Sometimes it takes 15 days or one or two months after the guy has arrived until he sleeps for the first time, works better and you hear him pray the Hail Mary, whether he believes or not; and then one day this guy looks into your eyes and says—THANK YOU! Thank you because you kept me here! Thank you because without you, I also would not be here, I would not be able to stand it. There is nothing on earth with which you could pay for this thank you and what you could exchange it for. There is no money with which you could pay for this thank you, the thank you that someone tells you, who was in the chains of the drug and begins to free himself from it.

I believe that the beauty of the community is that it is a school of life, a community, whose first goal is to help young people to meet God in their hearts. The beauty lies in the very fact that it embraces you in the beginning and accepts you undeservedly. It does not ask you if you have money in the bank, if you are black or white, if you are able to work, if you have studied something, it looks into your eyes and accepts you.

In our community, one does not pay for one's stay, one lives by divine providence. The community accepts, helps, invites, stimulates and teaches to love. And what one learns and what happens surpasses everything that we can have within us.

None of us, who have taken drugs, say when they enter. 'I believe.' But this is not what the community wants of you, it teaches you to pray. After prayer comes the faith. It does not say, 'Have faith, then pray,' but first, 'PRAY!' Sister Elvira forces us on our knees, 'PRAY, and then faith will come.' She does not ask you if you love, but she teaches you to be with Jesus. Then through sacrifice, love is born. The community does not teach through great speeches and catechism, but first teaches through life. It is true that Sister Elvira also speaks and teaches through catechism, but she teaches us to pray through prayer. She teaches us to bend our knees, but she is also the first one to kneel down herself. She teaches us to pray in front of Jesus, but she prays more than we, before we do so, and together with us. So, Sister Elvira speaks with us through life. Today, thank God, the life of the guys, who entered into the community before us and who are older than us, becomes our school.

Life, that renews itself, must have the desire to renew others, to work at renewing and to love. I can only say that I will remain in the community, in spite of everything that may go through my head, because I am being loved; but it is even more beautiful to love. It is really beautiful to do good to the others. Today I feel that Jesus did not only let me resurrect physically, but He also let my heart be resurrected. Now this is a heart that wants to love. For this, I always want to continuously thank God, who is our Father; I thank Him because He created me and put Sister Elvira on the path of my life.

4. RAFAELE SIGNORELLI

I am Rafaele. I am 24 years old. I find I am very happy because I am in the community. Without the community, I would have never stopped taking drugs. Before the community, I had chosen death. I took drugs, I did not have the will to stop. A couple of times I tried it alone, but I could not go on without drugs. I fell again and again. In the community, I discovered the joy of life, which I had never felt before. If I had to say why I took drugs, there were many things responsible: curiosity, false friends, I had too much of everything. But most of all, I was responsible. I always knew what I was doing. It is not true that the one, who takes drugs, does not know what he is doing. At every moment, I knew what I did. My conscience spoke, the voice of goodness was within me, but my voice was much stronger. I know now, the real reason for my taking drugs, was my inability to live. This is the true, deep reason and no one else should be accused.

I grew up in a simple, honest family and I cannot say anything bad about my family. My family always got along well, they had problems with no one. My parents loved me in the best sense of the word. They gave me everything that they had not had. I often heard my mother and father say they wanted to give me everything they never had. I grew up in all this, but within me, I became more and more empty. I also became full of pride.

What I had was not enough for me, I always wanted more and my parents gave it to me. I was not born into a rich family. My parents made many sacrifices for me. They thought they would make me happy by putting money in the bank for me, by promising me a house when I get married. They wanted to offer me a secure future without worries and without my own efforts. They wanted to do this instead of me. While thinking too much about TOMORROW, they forgot about TODAY. My parents worked during the day and at night they were tired. There was no time to be together. There was no communication and one did not ask for forgiveness when quarrelling. These all seem to be only small things, but they are important. I lost trust in my parents. They wanted me to make a good impression on everyone and in everything I did. For example, when I was not good in school, the main problem was WHAT ARE THE OTHERS THINKING?! I always wanted to be dressed well because it was important to me what the others might think.

When I was 14, I already had to learn to make decisions. My decisions, however, were not in agreement with the will of my parents. I did what I wanted. I began to contradict my parents and had no trust in what they were trying to teach me. So I began to be with older friends in order to feel important, to feel more grown up and to do big things. I carried a lot of money in my pocket. I often went out at night. In the meantime, I gradually lost the true values of life, like friendships. I thought, if you wanted to have someone as your friend, it meant to give something to him, but also to have something. I always expected something in return. I was a person, who was never ready to make a sacrifice because my parents had given me everything. I also lost the right attitude for the meaning of freedom. I thought that freedom meant to do what you want, to come and go when you want, not to have to tell anyone what you have been doing, not to need anything from anyone. I saw this with my friends. I also did this and thought that I was smarter than those of my own age.

Then I began to smoke marijuana. I began with this drug out of curiosity. When I began to smoke, I was an empty and destroyed human being. When I smoked marijuana, I did not think I was a drug addict because it did not make me physically dependent. Then I began to steal. I always said that I would never become like the others. I never thought that I would become a drug addict like the others. I wanted to remain with marijuana and only smoke when I wanted to and when I was with my friends. But it was not so. I took more and more heavy drugs until I started with heroin. I took heroin for five years. These were very hard years and I wanted to quit.

My mother discovered my problem right away. She began to care for me even before I started to take drugs. I also started stealing money from my house before taking drugs. Because of the drugs, I began to steal continuously and took everything that could be sold out of the house and sold it. My mother realized immediately what was happening to me, even though she did not accept it. I also asked myself what the others thought of me, this interested and worried me. My father also asked himself frequently what the others would think, if they found out that his son was taking drugs. I was avoiding the eye contact of others. I did this because I was afraid that the others would discover my addiction and would ask me to stop taking drugs. But I only had one need, to continue to take drugs.

The years of taking drugs were years of pain for me and my family. Drugs brought deep unrest into my life and that of my family. My parents were very disappointed with what I was doing. My parents spent a lot of money for my therapy. They were always with me. But they hid everything from the others. I sometimes took advantage of the situation. One day my mother said to me, "Now it is enough! You have to go into the community. We are no longer able to help you!"

When I heard this, I left the house and began to live alone, which meant living on the street. I remained for sometime outside of the family and then came the disappointment. It was very difficult. No one gave me anything to eat, to drink, I also could not sleep. My mother told everyone I was taking drugs; and that is why everyone behaved accordingly. Then I remained totally alone. I asked my mother if she could help me. She told me again that I should go into the community and I accepted it, not because I wanted it, but because I was completely disillusioned. I did not know where to go.

I can only thank my parents that I am in the community today because, had it been up to me, I would have never entered. When I came into the community, it was very difficult for me to accept what the community was offering, especially because I thought that the drugs were my problem. It was difficult for me to be with the others, to do without things, to listen, to accept what others were doing for me, not to be with those, with whom I wanted to be, and not be able to do what I wanted to do. Drugs were not my problem. I became aware that these were really my problems. In the beginning, it was really difficult to accept that. I also had to work but I was not used to that. I had to pray but during my whole life, I had never accepted prayer.

Once I said to Sister Elvira that I would do everything she wanted of me but I would not go into the chapel. To that, Sister Elvira said, "You don't need to go into the chapel, but you go to work!" I was not told, "sleep until 8 am, then go to work" or "wait in front of the chapel and then go to work." I was told, "go to work immediately." After a couple of days, I was exhausted from work. I did not feel well physically. I remember one morning when I said to the guy, who was with me, "Take me with you into the chapel, I want to rest!" I did this out of the desire for comfort.

No one from the community asked my parents for money, they did not ask me what work I could do, about my diploma from school, or if I believed or not. They accepted me as I was and this was beautiful for me. I always had wanted people to love me as I was and for what I had, for what one could see from the outside and not for what is inside. Although they accepted me and loved me, I thought each day that I could no longer stand it and that I would leave the community. But I found the persons, who were ready to listen to me, to forgive me, to help me to begin anew, persons who gave me their time. What kept me in the community in the beginning, was this friendship because I believed neither in myself nor in the community.

In the evening, I was always satisified with what I had done and in the morning, I began the day without any will and any courage. Many jobs were a great sacrifice for me. These were really my first victories and after the sacrifice of the job, I felt good. Then I began to love the others. I have always had problems to show the others that I meant well. Today I no longer have this problem. I can say that I love them.

I feel that I need the community and I still want to remain here. I really feel that I have become a new person, although I know I am still weak. The problem I have is not the work, or leaving the community or the fear of a sacrifice, but my biggest fear is that I will return to drugs. I also feel a fear of women, even though I feel strong and want to move ahead. I have realized that when I want to feel well, I have to love someone. And when I want to feel well, then I must help the others so that they feel well. The greatest treasure the community has put into my hands is that I wish the others well and want to do good things for them. When I entered into the community, I did not believe that this was possible but today I believe it and know it. Today I can sacrifice time for others and I know how important it is. I also learned to love the truth and to have the strengh to say the truth and that is to tell the others how I really feel inside. Today I believe in this and it builds me up. I do not experience the community as a hospital or prison because the prison can only be within me and there are people around me, who love me and whom I love. Now I have so many friends and this is the real treasure.

The community has taught me to pray, even when I don't have the desire to do so, when I am tired or did not sleep enough or when I have a headache or another excuse. Today I pray in spite of all the difficulties. I have already learned to kneel down and pray in the morning at 6 am and in the evening at 7pm. It is not difficult for me to go into the chapel alone to pray and to listen to the voice of my conscience. I have the strength to be good, although I am not perfect yet. When I go to sleep, I have the strength to look for forgiveness, for reconciliation, even if I know it is not my fault. Prayer gives me the strength to listen to the voice within me. Each time when I don't have the strength to listen to my conscience, I feel badly and I don't have the strength to look into the eyes of the others. I cannot remain indifferent to the voice of my conscience. When I search my conscience and look for forgiveness, I feel how Jesus forgives me and peace returns to me.

As far as confession is concerned, it is very important to me to admit sin and look for forgiveness. Sometimes things disturb me that I have already confessed. I am not afraid to admit them and to ask for forgiveness. I am no longer afraid of confession, no matter what I have done. This is very important for me because I know how afraid I was to admit my sins. I don't really want to know how it happened that I was able to free myself from all my fears. What is important for me and what I want is to live these things. It is not diffiuclt for me to forgive those, who brought me into drugs, and it is not difficult for me to ask those for forgiveness, to whom I have done evil to, because of the drugs....much evil. Today I am not ashamed to talk about these things, although it is difficult for me. This happens because I know that everything is being forgiven. As far as my parents are concerned, our relationship has changed completely. Today I can thank them for life and for all the sacrifices they have made for me. I can say thank you to my mother because she ironed my shirt, I can tell her that I love her. I can say thank you to my father because he has given me money. I have never done this before. And if we quarrel today for one reason or another, it is not difficult for me to ask for forgiveness and reconcile.

I know that I did not accept my mother as she was. I also feel that my parents have forgiven me for all the evil things I have done to them. The fruits, which I carry in my heart, are really numerous. On the one hand, I want to be in the community, but on the other hand, I want to be with my parents. I am ready to go into another community, I am also ready to leave, to meet a girl and to start a family. Nothing is difficult for me. I have realized that it is not important, where I am or what I do, but it is only important that I have inner peace.

5. BORIS VIDOVIĆ

I am Boris Vidović. I am 27 years old. I have been in the community for four years.

I was born in Split. I have a father, mother and brother. We are a normal Catholic family. The first things, which I remember, are from elementary school. They were fears and problems because of physical deficiencies. I was afraid that the children would laugh at me, that they would think bad things about me. Those were my complexes. They became a part of my life. I remember that I never spoke to anyone about these things, either with friends or with my family. They were hidden inside me, they were the secrets I kept in order not to show my weakness. At the same time, I began to fight against this but, unfortunately, in the wrong way. I did it, by taking advantage of the weaknesses of others and laughing about them. I was intelligent and clever, like many others. I was not hard working, I was not one of the best but, in any case, I was a good student. Already in the 5th or 6th class, I don't remember exactly, I wanted to show off with other things, I wanted to be in the center of attention, so that others would laugh about the things I said. I wanted to be with older boys from the 7th and 8th class, who became my idols, who stayed out longer, who smoked cigarettes, who already had girl friends, who were idols for me. I thought, if I became like them, I could solve my problems and then I would be satisfied. When I entered high school, this was a new world for me. Elementary school had been close to my home, so I did not know the town or the center of town. There I met guys and girls from all over. Then came puberty with its problems, the need to show off; I was more concerned about how I looked than anything else. The first time I went out, it was harmless. In going out the first few times, I began to become aware of my surroundings. I saw that there were drugs and discotheques. Everything was too soon for me. I remember, the first time I went into a disco, I was afraid. But I saw friends, who went there frequently. They had no problems approaching girls, they had no problems drinking beer. I was afraid to dance and to even talk to a girl. The same fears, the same complexes and the same shyness all came out. I remember that I became more and more reserved and so not much remained of the small boy from elementary school, who always knew how to be in the center to attract attention, who was always ready for a good joke and laugh. Somehow my problems became a part of me. I did not know that there was a possibility to talk to someone about them. With my friends I talked more about others, we gossiped and laughed about those, who went to church; we thought that those, who studied and who tried hard, were foolish and backward because we had already discovered pleasures, about which they knew nothing, and so we felt more intelligent than they. The clique I hung around with went from bad to worse and I looked exaclty for these kinds of cliques. Other good friends of mine also became worse and worse. So the foundation for drugs was laid. Already then

I met some drug addicts and drug dealers. They were those, who had money, motorbikes and girls. To me, they seemed content because they had everything and, in their way of life and in their freedom, these older guys were somehow idols for me. I thought I would never take drugs but these guys came closer and closer and I was drawn closer and closer to them. Then began the lies in the family. Earlier the lies had been in connection with school and friends, but now they became dangerous and critical. Because of the lies and my reservedness in front of my parents, I did not feel comfortable at home and the older I got, the more freedom I allowed myself and my parents somehow let it happen. I used every moment to go out. During the first year, I was not interested in high school, so I did not use much time to learn and to make it through school.

Then the first harmless stealing began. Slowly I lost my peace. I returned home with my fears that someone would notice or discover something. My parents asked me where I had been. I answered, "Outside." "Who were you with?" I answered, "with friends" (whom they knew and whom they trusted). I always mentioned names that gave them confidence. But the parents began to notice that I was going with friends, who were not good. Then I started stealing with my friends, which shocked my family. The drugs were not there yet, but the police and lawsuits were there already. Since I was not of age, I was not severely punished. A social worker had to watch over me. My family had its first shock. They saw for the first time that the road I had taken was not good. Then I became frightened because I also saw that it was not good and that I would have to change something. I signed up for Merchant Marine School because it interested me. Slowly plans for the future developed in me. During the first two years in school, I tried quite hard. The drug was already there but they were only light drugs. I did not think this was dangerous, I thought it was normal. For me this was a part of my freedom; because for me freedom meant to have what I wanted; to come back home when I wanted, to work in what I wanted, to go to discos, to earn money in the way I wanted . . . I already began with heavier drugs. The experience to earn my own money, which I earned easily, was very interesting to me. Again, I thought I was smarter than the others, I showed off, I enjoyed the fact that, in my clique, they thought I was someone, who could do something.

On the other hand, life within me was a complete disappointment. I was unable to converse, unable to forgive and to reconcile with others. I remained more and more alone, my circle of friends became smaller and smaller and finally they were only those, who could be with me only because they did what I did. Then came my first experiences with heroin. After having taken lighter drugs, it was not difficult for me to force myself to the next step, to heroin. When my friends began to talk me into taking heroin, it did not take them long to persuade me. Above all, this drug deceived me, like the other drugs. First I thought I would not be like the others and that is why I could try it because nothing would happen, I would not become addicted because I was not like the others. These are thousands of excuses we drug addicts use. Finally, heroin became a need for the solving of my problems. Neither marijuana nor any other ligher drug could solve my problems. I tried to solve all my problems in the wrong way. Heroin seemed a solution for everything. I felt that I was one with those, who took drugs with me, because we had something that no one knew anything about it, we had our secrets, together we felt strong. For the first time, I felt what friendship is, to share the things that unite us. But this feeling, that I had found something for my life, lasted only a short time. I became an addict. The worse my inner state became, the easier it was for me to become an addict. I was pulled into the stream of drugs that sucked me with it. I needed a lot of money to be able to take drugs every day. When I had succeeded for today, I had to worry already about tomorrow. Each morning when I woke up, I thought about the drug, then about the money and this was how it was day in and day out. Life went on. I did not feel like a drug addict because I continued to go into discos and I seemed normal to the others. I often saw drug addicts, who were stealing in town, who were unkept and untidy. I wasn't so. In this way I justified myself but only up to the day I had fallen so low that I began to steal. Heroin had destroyed me. At one moment heroin gave me the feeling of indifference and that everything was ok and, in the next moment, my disappointment increased. I realized that I could not stop anymore. While taking drugs, I often saw young men, who did not take drugs, who were successful in life, who worked and owned things and who were respected. I began to envy them and felt jealousy. I had enough energy and the desire to stop was strong. I tried it a hundred times. I had begun to work before taking heroin. I worked on boats. To go to work meant not to take drugs for a time, but only for a certain amount of time. Each time when I stopped for awhile, I had the hope that everything was over and that everything was ok, but after a few months everything was, as it had been before, but only worse. My fears became stronger and stronger and my problems overwhelming and more difficult. I stopped going out. I had no interest in anything, neither pleasures nor discos. I had no more interest in anything that I believed had become part of my life. I was only interested in the drug.

As far as my friends were concerned, I used them when I needed them or they used me. When I could use a girl for money or for my own selfish ends, when I could use my family, I did it. The desire to stop taking drugs did not stop. I remember, since childhood I had the wish not to take drugs and not to live badly. I had the wish to work and to lead a good life, I had several ambitions. You know, I had gone to Merchant Marine School. I liked that job, I liked to work on ships. People were satisfied with my work, they respected me, but the drug was much stronger. The evil had won. The good within me was not strong enough. I could not remain good.

It became clear to me that I needed help. My family knew that I was taking drugs. They were looking for help, which I did not accept. I accepted the help of a doctor, who gave me methadone, which is also a drug. He freed me from physical dependency but, whenever I had a chance to take drugs, I took them. I started to have health problems with my liver. I had to go to the hospital twice. My friends and girlfriends began to die from the drugs. Some landed in jail. The worst thing that could have happened with drugs did; death began. At that time, I was afraid of drugs. It was not like in the beginning. It was not beautiful anymore. It became a necessity for life. I could not eat anymore without having taken drugs before. In order to get out of bed and go to sleep, I had to take drugs. It simply became a necessity for my life.

I remember that I had already spoken sometime before with the psychologists of Sister Bernardica about entering a community in Italy. At that time, I thought this was not necessary for me. I thought I could do it myself, although I knew that no one had been able to stop taking drugs on his own. No one has succeeded forever. Maybe someone succeeded for a short period of time or took another drug or alcohol instead, but the drug always remains. It was in me.

My parents began to go to a prayer group. In the Church of St. Peter in Split, the parents of addicts met. They did this for sometime, I don't remember exactly for how long.

They tried to persuade me to do something; then they began to talk more and more about the community and about my going there. Also my friends and I on the street talked about the communities because a few had gone and returned and were taking drugs again. I did not even know what a community was. One thing was clear: I was afraid. I was afraid to go anywhere, where I would not be able to have my own will, where I had to live like the others wanted me to. The last possiblity, which I wanted to think about, was the community.

Then, shortly before my entering into the community, it happened that several friends and I began selling heroin and drugs. We had a lot of money and we were always together. This gave me hope. Life became beautiful for me again— friends, money, girls—I did again what I wanted to do, thought I was better than the others, who had nothing and who had to earn money. Before that, I had left my job because I no longer had the strength to work. But soon everything was over. We had used up the money very quickly. Then again came a time, which was very hard for me and oppressive. Since I was an addict, my need was great. I took Heptanon. I began to make and have debts, began to cheat often, began the life on the street, a life that was a fight for every penny in order to be able to buy drugs.

I remember when a friend from my childhood came from Germany. I wanted to break into his apartment several times. He was a friend, who was really good to me but I had fallen so low that I did not care about anything; anything was permitted to get drugs. The situation with my friend came to a peak because everyone found out how I really was; but they really had already known it before. All neighbors had known it. The disappointment within me grew. I did not feel free anymore to walk in front of my house, to meet someone and to look into the eyes of people, who thought that there was still hope. I quarrelled with my friends. I began to think about what I should do. My parents took advantage of this situation, but not only they, also my brother and all, who wanted the best for me; they suggested the community to me. They tried, in one way, to persuade, to force me into the community. My parents did not throw me out of the house, but I know they would have done so, because they saw that I was slowly dying. It became terrible. I began to go to the meetings in the community in Medjugorje.

On the whole, the first meeting in the community was for me something I had never seen before. I saw young people, who worked. I remember, there was a guy named Toni, who told me about the community. The words he used at the time were words from a different world, words I had never heard before, especially not from someone, who had previously taken drugs. I distrusted him and others. When I heard that in the community, no cigarettes, no TV, not this, not that, were allowed, I had enough reasons not to go into that community. The drug was stronger than I. The situation at home, the relationship with my parents—all this pushed me into the community. Also my problems with the police because of stealing and because of everything else I had done, helped me to enter into the community. My entrance came about because of two things: on the one hand, because of the police, on the other, because of my inner condition of fear and disappointment. In the community, however, hope began to rise in me when I watched the guys and so I entered into the community in Ugljane (near Split). There I spent the first four to five months. Then I went into the community in Italy, where I remained approximately one year and then I returned again to Croatia. The community is a place, where you give up many things; but I could not understand what this was all good for, what it was really about. For me, the community was work and prayer. I soon realized that the community is really something completely different. I had the same problems as I had outside, like in my childhood, the same fears and complexes. It was all the same. But the ways and means to solve them, as

I had done before, did not exist; my own room did not exist, where I could lock myself in and listen to music; the drug did not exist; my friends did not exist, with whom I had talked about superficial things in order to forget my problems. There was no TV or newspapers, nothing. All this made me afraid.

I realized that I could not live. I had to accept the failure of my life and that is exactly what is not easy. It takes time. Maybe I still make mistakes in certain things today. In fact, however, I know in that moment, when I told myself the truth—that I had taken the wrong road and that I wanted to learn to live—I have remained in the community and decided to stay, in spite of the fears and the millions of difficulties and problems with others and myself.

With the help of the others, who were next to me and remained steadfast, the guys who had lived through the same experiences I had gone through and still do, I will see it through. The beginning was difficult, but I was also content because I felt the community was right for me. I was neither treated like a patient nor like a backward person, but I was accepted as a young person, who needs love, friendship and dialogue.

So at that time, I did not realize the things I talk about now. At that time I did not understand many things. The guys told me, "Even though you don't understand, believe what we tell you." I trusted my friends, who were different from those on the street. They kept me with them. They were the true friends, who led me on the right path, their shoulders were not there so that I could cry on them, but showed me the way to salvation.

I got to know prayer. Prayer for me was nothing special. I come from a Christian family and as a child I went to religion classes. Before it was normal for me to say that I believed in God, but, in reality, my life had no connection with God. I got to know another form of prayer—guys, who pray the rosary morning and evening. Everything was strange for me, although I cannot say that I did not want to believe. Already from the beginning, I also wanted to pray. The others showed me the way; especially helpful were the things I heard from Sister Elvira, which I also hear today from other people, who have great faith. The longer I am in the community, the more experience I have, the more examples, the more prayer. Today I understand that the community is not a place, where one works, where you learn this or that, but the community has really brought me and all others closer to Jesus. After a long time in the community, I also began with personal moments of prayer. For the first time, I began to pray on my own. For the first time, I felt that someone was with me and gave me help that is not from man. I began to realize that there is a Lord and that there are holy things. This was the beginning of my Christian path. But I know—the community is the one that shows me this path. Our community is large because it is not afraid to tell the truth, it does not promise a young guy to heal him from drugs, but the community told me, "If you don't want to take drugs, you have to change your life." This was exactly what made me afraid in the beginning and the feeling still makes me afraid sometimes now that I could lose my 'freedom', that I thought was freedom, and which still comes up in my mind at times. I thought freedom was to decide about oneself, to do things your own way, and to solve problems with your head; but now I see that there is another path, that the path is in trust, in providence and in faith. This is what the community has given me. The most important thing the community has given me, is the realization that I can do good, that also I can help someone, even if only in the smallest gestures, the smallest attention; I can talk with someone, do something for someone. It took me a long time to realize that it is a real enjoyment: to forget oneself, to forget your own problems that plague you, to forget your own past, which comes back in your thoughts and, which I often cannot control. Usually these thoughts plague me on days when I have no will or strength to go forward. Today I realize that there exists a sort of battle against this. There is prayer and, following that, the concrete life, when I devote time to myself and others, when I talk to others about my problems so that they can understand their problems. The most beautiful feeling in the community is when you have the opportunity to be with a guy, who has just arrived, when you have to explain things to him that you sometimes don't believe yourself, when you have to be mother and father to him, when you have to ask for forgiveness even though you are right, when you have to remain awake, when you are nervous because of him. Only then, you begin to understand what love is, only then do you realize that also your parents have wished this for you, that they had done what they could. These are the things, which the community taught me since I am here.

It is a great thing how the relationships in my family have changed, where there had been no communication between me and my parents, even though there were many positive things. Had my family had not been, I also would not be here. Of course, there were also many difficulties and problems in my family like in any other. This does not mean that they were the reason I took drugs. In my family, we reconciled with each other; we want to do something for a better tomorrow; I want that my parents and I become friends. I remember when my father came into the community and remained with me. Those were days, in which we talked about our entire life, about all the things that were between us. We talked, we became friends. The community has made this possible for me. Although I came destroyed, disappointed and inwardly bad, the community saw something good in me and also sees my talents today, but also the difficulties and helps me to get rid of them. Sometimes it seems to me as if all this were not true; everyday problems arise all the time and the more I go forward, the more I return to those problems, which I have had since my childhood. But today I solve them in another manner and that is in the way the community teaches me. When I will leave the community and, should I take the same road I took before, when I will start to think not to take drugs anymore and permit myself certain things, for example, to be with one foot in the good and the other in evil, then I know that I will not be successful. I know that before, this was not enough for me, I know it will not be enough for me tomorrow.

I am especially grateful to Sister Elivra for what she has done for me, for what she is still doing and for what she will be doing in the future. Life in the community is not for a certain length of time one spends here, it is a way of living, which I want to accept, in spite of all the difficulties. It is not always easy to talk to others about your own problems, one must forget oneself, which is often difficult. The community has shown me how it will be when I accept that. I don't know what more I could say except thank God, a great thank you to Sister Elvira and to the brothers, who since I have known them, have lived with me through everything beautiful and not so beautiful. I thank my parents, the priest Jure from Split and everyone, who has prayed for me. Those things, which I know today, seem normal to me and there is a danger that I become accustomed to them; but when I think about the time before the community—then a miracle happened, a resurrection, in which I want to believe today. That means I believe that there was always someone, who wanted to help me, but I did not want to accept the hand. Today I want to accept this hand and I want to believe that I have begun a new Christian life.

Today I feel neither smarter nor bigger than those, who still take drugs, but I feel happier because I am no longer in the hell of drugs.

Medjugorje, December 1996.

6. FRANCESCO TANTARDINI

I am Francesco. I was born in Italy, in the province of Lecco. I am 28 years old and have been living in the community for six years.

Like many guys, who are living with me, I also believe that I have found the joy of life because I have laid aside the cross of drugs.

I was only one year old when my parents put me in the care of my grandmother because they were busy with work in the restaurant. When I think of my childhood, I know that there were many beautiful things; I was a good boy. I was sensitive and I suffered when I saw that boys, who were physically and mentally weaker, were laughed at and ridiculed. I was also a generous boy. This is why many took advantage of me. Although my mother raised me as a Christian, I began very early to follow the example of older guys and was ashamed to be good because in the logic of many guys this means to be foolish; I wanted to be different, I wanted to be appreciated and accepted, I wanted to be similar to my idols whom I had created for myself through TV and music. Already then I was a drug addict!

I began to lie, to smoke my first cigarettes in secret, to stay away from school, to steal and to read pornographic magazines; I did not talk about this with anyone, except with the friends, whom I visited and who were always with me. I only saw my parents on Saturdays and Sundays. They asked me how I was and I always answered that I was well! I wanted to ask them for advice but, above all, I wanted to ask them if, in their youth, they had lived through what I was living through; but I did not want to show that I needed them, especially because I did not accept that I was the only son and the fact that they had put me under the care of my grandmother, even though I liked her very much. After having finished elementary school, I went to high school, I was very reserved and had an unstable character. I was envious of friends, who were open and successful in everything, who were not afraid to hear their own voice and to say what they thought, and who were not afraid to tease girls. When I smoked 'joints', I felt free. I thought I had finally found the means, with which I could conquer my fears and my shyness. I was still convinced that I could do what I wanted and be independent. I hated all those, who took drugs, and felt that I was not like them. I always said I would never use the needle, but when I was 17, I began to do just that. At this point, I also thought I had found a medicine to solve my problems and a means to be happy; but I soon convinced myself that this was not true. But it was already too late.

Heroin was in the first place in my thoughts from the early morning until late evening. I began to work, but soon the money I earned was not enough, as was also the money that I got from my parents and my relatives in a deceptive way. I was very disappointed because my only goal was to take drugs and I did this, knowing well that with an overdose, I would destroy my life. I had to steal every day in order to get the 'goods' and after having gotten them, I locked myself into the house. I turned into a larva.

At the age 22, I had to go into jail for a number of thefts and I was asked to make a choice to go either into prison or to the community. When I entered into the community, I was very self-conscious and I could not believe that so many guys, like myself, could be happy without drugs and without all those things that young people need today. I felt very uneasy about the fact that Sister Elvira did not put any pressure on me to go into the community and that she did not accept any money from the state. This helped me accept myself as I was and I felt that I was forgiven and loved.

I met many guys, who were very patient with me in spite of all my negative reactions; for example, when I had no motivation to work and when I wanted to send them to the devil. I asked myself how the others could handle this, from where they took their strength, the great joy, the great cheerfulness—that which I did not have. Soon I discovered that many got up during the night to pray alone and this I really wondered about. I took part in the communal prayer, when I had to, and thought this would be a way to strengthen my will.

I felt that I was slowly changing and I wanted to be good again, as I had been when I was small. The actual life in the community made me realize, and still does so today, which sacrifices my parents and my grandmother had made for me, so that I could mature; I felt how difficult it had been for my parents and grandmother to help me in my development. Only here it became clear to me how difficult it is to wash clothes, to clean the house, to work in the kitchen, to make the bed . . these were many small things but they were important; I only did them because I had to; I did not honor them, I was never thankful for them.

Today I know that my parents gave me everything in good will so that I would not be lacking anything they had not had; I am not accusing them, but I feel that I love them. I would not exchange them for any others.

Partly out of curiosity and partly because the other guys motivated me, I began to get up a half hour before the usual wake-up time in order to pray alone. I went in front of the most Holy Sacrament, even though I understood nothing (as I still don't understand it today). As I was praying in silence, many ugly things out of the past came into my mind, memories of when I had been stealing, had been violent, had taken drugs. I felt badly but I trusted in what Sister Elvira and the other guys, who were already longer in the community than I, told me—that Jesus heals in the Eucharist. Today I am totally convinced of that. I know that I can only understand and know myself when I am on my knees and that, in this way, I can only accept my limits and my poverty. I began to love myself and those close to me and so I began to feel the joy of life. This is an endless daily struggle because the evil is always waiting for me when I make a good step. Evil brings me back into my past and shows it to me, the evil wants me to lose my trust, but the mercy of God is great, and, thanks to confession and the talks with my brothers, I am always ready to begin anew. And this, for the entire life!

I am thankful to Sister Elvira and the community because they helped me to get to know the true face of God, the true Christian life and I thank God because He saved me by leading me into the community.

7. ENRICO SANGIORGIO

My name is Enrico. I was born 31 years ago in a village in the province of Turin.

I am a member of a large family, I have three sisters and three brothers. I am the third child and was spoiled by everyone. I remember the day of my first Communion well because my father died on this day. When this happened, I began to believe that all the beautiful things I had been taught were nothing more than a deception. Already then, I thought that there was no God and that they had lied to me about everything. I grew up and within me also grew my problems—the fears and desires that a child carries within. But I did not know to whom I could talk about this. I was ashamed of myself and embarrassed by what others might think of me. As time went by, I closed myself more and more. Already as a boy I was very active (I ran, I was loud, I played—maybe too much.) I discovered that behind my liveliness was the hidden fear to accept myself as I was. I was reserved, fearful, I was afraid to hear my own voice. In high school I began to reap the first fruits that my fears, reservedness and distrust had sown. At that time, I began to smoke my first cigarettes and when I held them in my fingers, I began to feel like a 'man'. But soon I also had to add alcohol, that gave me the strength to face life. Alcohol gave me the feeling of 'freedom'. To be free meant to me to do what I wanted, to have what I wanted, to return home when I wanted. Freedom meant to have everything that gave me independence. And so I decided to smoke the first 'joints' during a class excursion to Rome. These wrongdoings were means, with which I wanted to distinguish myself from others, who were 'persistently' leading a Christian life. I laughed at those, who went to Church or private chapels be-cause I thought this was totally useless; but in reality I was embarrassed because I did not have the courage to be like them—a simple guy, who accepts the reality of his life.

So I also came to heroin and with the first dose, I thought I had solved all my problems; I was no longer reserved, I had no more fears and with the girls I was open and was not afraid. The drug also gave me the strength to do all the things, which I had not been able to do without them. But soon I felt that heroin was ruining me inside and out and I felt that I was slowly but surely destroying myself, but I did not have the courage to look for help. Heroin became my only motive, sense and concern for life. Like many other addicts, I began to steal and to sell drugs because the money I earned was not enough. If I could not steal anything outside of my home, I stole from inside the house; I didn't think that I was actually stealing from my own family, which was suffering greatly, because I already had a brother, who was drug addicted. When my mother died, whom I liked very much, I accepted nothing that others said or suggested and this was a reason, I became rebellious from inside.

When I was 22, I decided to join a community and with the help of "Serta", I entered into a mixed community in which there were 13 boys and girls. I stayed a certain time with them but when I left them, I immediately started to take drugs again, and thus threw away everything that the others had tried so hard to develop within me. This new fall was a sign to me that it would be my fate to die one day of an overdose in a garden. Since I last had this thought, three years have passed and today I find myself in a reality, which is hard to describe in words. One can only live this reality. This is the community, the large family, that loves me each day, listens to me, teaches me and helps me every day to decide for myself to be good. It happens often that I say 'thank you' to heroin for the evil because through these sufferings, which I carried for a long time with pride, I discovered today the goodness, the mercy and the forgiving that God offers me, which I had given up soon after my first Holy Communion. God never left me, but He always remained close to me in order to bring me into the community that lives and wants to live, by offering to all disappointed and lost young people the certainty and hope that one can be resurrected through prayer. Today, in this life, I feel real because my main goal is to love and be loved and so to have freedom. Today freedom is very important to me, but not like I had imagined it before. Freedom means to have the courage to be in complete truth with oneself, to share one's own life with the others, to be at the disposal of others, in one word: to be ready to do everything for the benefit of others.

I want to surrender my life completely to God so that He can use me and realize His plans, which He, like a father, has prepared for me and I want to accept His will and not mine in my life. I can really say that I have found what I had so long been searching for and that is love, peace and joy. I was searching for all that and for myself but for a long time on the wrong paths and with the wrong means. So I had to meet a woman, who had the courage to tell me straight into the face, that I had failed in my life and that I had to start at point zero again so that I can build something, which is very strong and indestructible and that it is worthwhile to give everything for that. This woman is more than a mother, more than a sister, more than a friend.

This is Sister Elvira.

8. CLAUDIO MORABITO - WHO HAD A RELAPSE AND RETURNED

(One always asks a justified question: What happens when a guy completes his stay in the community? The success of a community is measured by the percentage of those, who continue to live a normal life. Here I bring an example which, in its own way, can open our eyes. The normal time for healing in the community is three years. From this example, we see that the time one spends in the community is relative. It is surely better to look for the right criteria for healing than to measure the days and years in the community. When the community decides that a guy is ready to cope with the realities of life, he can go; but still nothing is really certain. It is clear, someone, who was addicted, can be healed and someone, who was not, can become so; this is why also an addict, who has been healed, can fall again. From working with alcoholics, it is known that the time of abstinence is not important for a relapse. One says, that the first glass will, even after many years, be a glass without a bottom. This is why here the old rule applies: Resist at the beginning because the medicine is found late. Here I bring the story of a young man, who had been in the community, who left after his program was finished, then fell again, but also returned again. His example can help many to understand that one can neither give up nor become tired in the struggle for life.)

My name is Claudio. I am 39 years old. I grew up in a family that gave me Christian morals and values. I grew up superficially, my heart was not in the things that I learned. Because of the illness of my father, I had to spend part of my childhood with my grandmother from my mother's side. I did not receive much affection and love. The same was true with my parents. I thought they had no time for me. I returned to my family. I began to go to school. Already in early childhood my conflicts began. I did not want to study, so I began to work when I was 14 years old. When I was 16, I worked in a factory. Then I began to change my work and my outlook on life. I leaned toward the left politically, I accepted Marxist ideas. There was no dialogue, but not because my parents did not want it. I isolated myself more and more from them. After having finished my military service, I fell in love. That did not end well. Then I started to take heroin. The drug gave me the feeling that I was important. Each day I fell into a deeper crevasse, from which I could no longer come out by myself. From time to time, I was able to stop taking drugs, especially when I went on vacation with friends, who did not take drugs. But after having returned to Milano, the first thing I did was to take drugs. I remember when my mother saw me once taking drugs, she asked me why I was acting this way. I reproached her that she had not cared for me when I was small and that she should leave me in peace now to live my own life. After 10 years, which I spent taking drugs, my parents asked me to make a choice: either the community or the street. I chose the community, even though I was not completely convinced. During three years, I did everything that the community asked of me. When Sister Elvira gave me her complete trust and permitted me to leave the community, I was happy. I began a new life in a new city with two friends and lived according to other values of life. Soon after leaving the community, however, I felt again the fear that I would remain alone. I did not accept what the community had suggested, that is, I did not pray and did not go to Holy Mass. The fear increased and led me again into drugs. I had a complete relapse. After a few months, the friends, who were with me, helped me to talk to Sister Elvira. She took me back into the community.

The entrance back into the community was difficult. I was afraid of the criticism of my brothers. I spent a month in Saluzzo and then came to Medjugorje. Also here I felt no condemnation because of my relapse. They all accepted me and helped me. The most difficult thing was to forgive myself. After a good confession, I knew that the Lord had forgiven me. My parents, Sister Elvira and the community also forgave me. But I did not want to accept this mistake. Now, two years after my return, I learn again each day what it means to give oneself to others and to be selfless. Time does not change a person, but the person changes when he, himself, decides to change, by accepting prayer and sacrifice.

VI. WE HAVE SUFFERED
WITH THEM

Nobody suffers as much as the mother and the father when they meet their child, who is being controlled by drugs. Nobody can describe the pain and sorrow of the heart of the mother or the father when they see the destruction of life, which they had accepted and the ruination of all hopes they had for their child. But also nobody can be as happy as the parents when they see their child, returning from the world of slavery into the world of freedom, from the world of reservedness into the capability to communicate with others.

But how much does the one suffer, who has fallen into the evil and who goes through the valley of death, crying in vain for freedom, peace, hope, life, joy and togetherness?!

I, myself, have often severely judged the parents of addicts and the addicts themselves, but I was able to convince myself that this does not happen out of evil, but because of helplessness and ignorance. They are victims and one does not condemn victims!

Evil remains on the side of those, who use human woundedness and the human inclination to do evil as the basis to earn money!

OLGA AND GIANPIERO VASALLO

Gianpiero and Olga Vasallo from Bellinzago (Novara, Italy) came to visit their son, who is in the community of healed drug addicts. I wanted to find out from Dario's parents how they experienced the fact that their son took drugs. They were pleased to speak to me.

97

SB: You came to visit your son and you are staying several weeks in the community. Please tell us something about yourself first!

G+O: We are the parents of Dario. We have three children. Two daugthers are married, both have one child, they are happily married. Dario is our only son. Now we have more time and so we are doing apostolic work.

SB: Who is Dario and what happened to him?

G+O: Dario had always been a good son. We had no problems with him. We raised him like we did our daughters. He was always a little shy. In school, he was not the best pupil, but the teachers always praised him because he was a quiet and obedient pupil. At that time, we were glad he was shy and that we had no problems with him; so we also did not spend much time with him. I had a job and worked also in the house and my husband was a driver. We always had much work so my husband was not much at home and was rarely present. We worked because we also had debts since we had built a house. I often worked at home after dinner. The children helped each other and the sisters helped Dario, especially when there were problems at school. And so everything somehow continued in that manner in our family. We went to Holy Mass. Faith was a habit for us. Dario also went. There were no problems. He was and remained always reserved. When he had finished high school, we sent him to college. He soon returned because he was unhappy with his studies. He even accused us to have sent him without his own consent. He took on a job right away and was a diligent worker. In spite of all the changes, he remained reserved and with little will. However, I did not ask him about this. So everything continued.

SB: How could it be that he goes to college and you only find out later that he did not even want this?

G+O: At home we did not have many conversations. I must admit, since the daughters were much more open, I could talk to them as a mother and they glady talked to me about everything. But Dario was always reserved and hardly ever spoke. Even when we tried to talk with him, he usually only shrugged with his shoulders and was quiet.

SB: When and how did you discover the story with the drugs?

G+O: I saw that he went with a clique, which I did not like. I told him that I did not like his clique and that I was afraid. He was angry and promised to change his clique. He did this, but he always chose friends, who were even worse. We knew that he smoked marijuana, but I did not concern myself much with it, and I hoped that he would stop one day. But I deceived myself bitterly. From day to day, things got worse. Everything continued up to the day, when we, parents, accidently discovered the bitter truth about our Dario. We cleaned the house more thoroughly than usual and found a needle, a spoon and other sure signs that Dario was taking heavy drugs. We were both very shocked. Suddenly the whole world collapsed for us. We did not know what to do. When we confronted him, he answered with convincing assuredness that those were not his things and that he did not know who, had put them there. The two of us had never been in contact with such things; we did not know what drugs actually were and what that meant. We did not know that addicts can lie skillfully and that they are not afraid to lie, so that he was able to calm us down when he spoke so convincingly. Since he became more reserved, more quiet, more nervous, we sent him to the psychologist. He saw him for almost an entire year. However, there was no progress.

SB: What did you try after the psychologist?

G+O: We were in distress. We made the suggestion, which he accepted, that he spend some time with his sisters, who lived in another town, in order to leave his clique. However, this brought no result. We asked the psychologist for advice. He suggested 'stronger measures' against Dario. So we took away his car. This didn't matter to him at all. He was still going to work and his friends drove him there. After a certain time, we consulted the psychologist again and he said that we could give him back the car and a certain amount of money since everything was alright. We did this. And this was the mistake, the terrible, disastrous and deadly mistake. We discovered that he had had a relapse and, for me, this was the end of the world. I was constantly nervous, irritated, disappointed and sad. Everything was mixed up. I remember, once when we were together at home and my husband was not there, we were having dinner and then Dario said that he had go out. Since I was sure he wanted to go in order to take drugs, I did not want him to go. We quarrelled. Then he said to me, "I must go so I can use drugs because I don't, I won't be able to go to work tomorrow."

SB: Did you give in?

G+O: Yes. My husband was not at home. Dario went out and came back after one hour. He looked terrible. His stare was totally forlorn, he was stuttering. He was very pale. Not any different than a living dead. For me, that was terrible. I called a community, that accepts addicts, and told them everything I had heard and what I had experienced. The person in charge told me that it was always this way with addicts when they take drugs and he was surprised that I had only noticed it then for the first time.

Then, we, parents, took him again to the psychologist. Dario was always without a will. After that, we did not allow him to go out for sometime. He stayed with us and slowly became better. We slowly regained hope, but then he said again, he wanted to leave home. He did not want to go into a community. We were shocked, we tried to keep him back; we pleaded with him to stay, but everything was in vain. He got dressed, he simply took his sleeping bag and left. He was gone for three months. I did not see him once. Had I seen him, I don't know what I would have done. My husband and I kept on going to the psychologist for further talks. Dario withdrew his savings from the bank. He bought himself a car and slept in it. When he got some money from anywhere, he disappeared again.

Once he came home, he was only skin and bones. I hoped he had changed his mind. His father spoke with him a long time. Suddenly he began to cry and asked us, "Take me, I can't go on anymore!" Then he accepted to go into Sister Elvira's community.

SB: How did you react as parents?

G+O: For us, this was the happiest day and now we are here. He looks very well. We will remain here for a certain time. We have not yet begun to actually talk. It is difficult for him, as well as for us. Two years and three months have passed. Everything has turned for the better. But it takes time.

SB: If you could turn back time, after all these difficult and sad experiences, what would you do in order to avoid it?

G+O: One thing is certain—I would have more time for him. Had we again a son, who was as reserved, we would do everything in order to understand what happens in his heart; however, we did not do this.

SB: Did you know what happens in connnection with drugs?

G+O: We knew nothing about it. We knew nothing about addictions, nothing about how addicts behave; I did not think about the illnesses that resulted from it. Now it is clear to me that I sometimes wanted to do something; but my husband always found excuses and justifications, like work, stress, tiredness so that we did nothing even when we noticed something and had our doubts. My husband often said, "If I would know that my son takes drugs, I would kill him!" But when we discovered it, we lost all hope, we tried to help and discovered our helplessness. What we tried was wrong: to take him to the psychologist, to send him to his sisters' families, to forbid him to go out, nothing helped.

SB: How long did it take you to discover he took drugs?

G+O: We already knew in 1985 that he took light drugs. We knew about an incident with the police, but I did not think it was a serious matter. We gave him a lesson and hoped that he had understood it, but it was not so. He continued with his behavior. He never felt at ease at home. He told me this here, a couple of days ago, "I went out because there was nothing at home, no conversations, no true understanding, there was only work, TV and materialistic worries." Now we feel responsible for everything, because all our hopes were buried by the behavior of our son and because he suffered so much.

Thank God, we found Sister Elvira. She not only helps our son, but also us, as a couple. It is terrible when your child disappoints you and tears down everything, you tried to built up for him. And you feel that he is ready to destroy everything, to sell everything, even us. Now we also need a healing. Now we realize that one really has to pray at home, to go to Holy Mass, to talk with each other and to forgive one another. We have learned all this now.

We have realized that it is wrong to strive so hard in order that the children have everything, as far as material things are concerned.

One should also consciously show them many values of life and point out that everything they have, someone had to earn and someone had sweated for. One must learn to live with God, then we can live with each other, we will be able to be honest and sincere with the others, love and forgive them.

SB: Now, when looking at everything, can you justify your views at the time?

G+O: Before we lived through this catastrophe, we had a justification why we had no time for our children—because we worked so much. Now I know that there is no justification here. When our children need us, then we should be with them because, when this period of time in their education has passed, one cannot bring it back, but the negative consequences remain. The child does not understand, he needs the presence of his parents and when the parents are not present, the child suffers. We did not realize this. We used to say, "What more do you want of us, we are working for you until we are worn out, you have everything!?" O, how naive this was!!

SB: The time you spent with your children, how did you spend it?

G+O: When we were together, the television was turned on, we watched the news and movies, we said nothing and only watched television. After that, we were tired and we went to bed. There was no conversation and no true friendship.

If we could bring back this time, we would do things differently and no one would need to go hungry and dress indecently. We deluded ourselves and this has cost us dearly. Also our daughters were very disappointed. They cried much, they tried to help him.

For us, this is inner pain. We raised them all in the same manner and the daughters are really good, well-behaved women, they have families, they are good wives and mothers. Dario was looking for something else.

SB: What have you learned by your visits in the community?

G+O: We have learned many things. One can live with much less. One should be open and speak with one another. One should really pray, prayer changes life and the interpersonal relationships. Then there is neither anger nor hate and one forgives immediately. We have learned to accept our weaknesses and faults and not be ashamed of them. When we, as parents try to hide them, we, as well the children suffer. Here we have learned the basic things.

SB: How do you see the situations in the families now, the relationships between the parents and the youth? Say something for everyone!

G+O: The situation is bad. Many make the same mistakes as we did. May God save them from similar sorrows! So our message for all parents would be: pray with your children, speak with them, be near to your children, teach them to be ready to make large and small sacrifices. And when you see that your child has gotten himself into difficulties, don't make any new mistakes, as we did.

Don't accuse anyone, neither society nor the Church, no one. Parents, you must realize that everything depends on you. In the beginning it is easy to stop everything, but, once your child has already become an addict, lead him into the community. Open your eyes, recognize what happens through his behavior and be near to your children. When the children are nervous and always tired, when they continuously need money, then start having your doubts and help them. May our Lord protect you from evil! Peace be with you!

MOTHER CONTE

I am thankful to my drug-addicted son because through him, I met Sister Elvira and the community 'Cenacolo'. I am also thankful to drugs because throught it I began to implore the Holy Spirit. How many more steps must I take in order to begin to live faith? Surely many. For a long time, I had completely neglected the Holy Spirit because I thought it was not important. What was important was the material security and I did not have many problems to think about. My children were already grown and were able to take care of themselves.

I did not worry about their souls. Drugs had to come. I think of the cross, which we all have to bear, but which we left somewhere on the road. I had forgotten the cross completely, I let the others carry it for me. What a mistake and what care-lessness on my part! Who am I? Now, when I have to ask this question, I understand that the only answer is: I am a com-plete failure! At the same time, I have a true and single hope that I can begin again, that I can always better myself, while finally learning to pray to Jesus with my whole heart and to ask Him for forgiveness on my knees.

The meeting with the parents, that Sister Elvira has orga-nized, was very beautiful and interesting, because it gave us great peace and cheerfulness and invited us to live in truth. During the three days of the meeting, which she directed with Charile, we spoke with the other parents and prayed together and we exchanged testimonies. I feel that I not only love the parents that I already knew, but also all, whom I met for the first time. I feel as if I were in a large family in which we, while holding hands, all search for the help of the Holy Spirit and pray with greater and greater trust that He hears us. The strength of the faith of Sister Elvira touches us deeply and I have realized how much time I have lost, since the time I put my faith aside, convinced that it was enough to believe and it was not important to practice the faith.

I want to ask forgiveness from everyone because I was very often self-centered. I thought that I always had to be among the first and looked with disdain on some parents, who had come into the community for the same reasons as I. I judged them rather than helping them with my testimony, as the others were helping me.

Slowly, I discover the joy of life and feel myself to be among the last, even though before the Lord we are all equal. I repeat again, "Thank you drugs, because, through you and through Luka, who searched for you and took you, I have discovered

my frightening shortcomings and the mistakes I have made."
The community 'Cenacolo', helps me to discover my mistakes
and I also feel that it will help me in the coming days, because
we now have the power of faith—the faith in the Resurrection!

VINKO BUDIŠA

I am happy I am able to welcome you all, and want to
emphasize at the start that I did not come here so that you can
see me, I didn't come to publize myself and my family. But I
am here at the invitation of your priest and because I feel the
need to help the parents, who fear drugs. We know from experience that those, who are able to help the most, are those,
who have had this hell in their own family and have experienced this hell in their own bodies. This is why I ask you, dear
parents, let us begin, as soon as possible, to help each other
and we will have the opportunity to help those near to us, our
brothers, our neighbors and—may God forbid—one day also
our own child. One can best help with the truth. When we say
the truth, we first help ourselves because we express what
bothers us and so also help others to listen to us. This is why
I shall speak completely open with you tonight and without
being ashamed of myself and my family.

My name is Vinko Budiša and this is my wife, Maja. I am 48
years old and we have been married for 25 years. Children
did not force us to get married. We had them because we
wanted them. We got married because we loved each other
and were convinced that we were right for each other. Then
the first child came. This is my son, Gordan, who is 24 years
old today. I have to tell you when Gordan was born, we were
really the happiest parents. We wanted to give him everything
that parents can give a child. Four years later, we had a second child. We were not surprised. We wanted the child. We
treated him like the first child. We wanted to educate our chil-

dren so that they would be honest human beings. We wanted them to become persons, whom we would not have to be ashamed of one day. We also tried to live in a way so that our children would not have to be ashamed of us.

In my home, there was no alcohol, no conflicts, no physical violence, no stealing. From day to day we tried to instill the qualities we both had into our children. We were always together with our children. We did not spend one weekend without them. When you hear this, you will think we were a good family. But in my family, there was an addict. My oldest son began to take drugs when he was 15 years old. We, the parents, did not recognize this immediately. It took us a long time to discover the truth about him. When we realized he was an addict—and both of us had feared drugs the most—only a trace of our harmonious life remained. True hell began. It is unbelievably difficult to experience drugs in your own home. Although my wife and I are quite similar in our way of thinking, we began to quarrel and unrest came between us.

We accused each other. Nevertheless, thanks to our cooperation and mutual understanding, we were soon able to overcome these misunderstandings because we realized we could not save our son in this way. Father and mother cannot save their child, but only the entire family. Unfortunately, we did not have the opportunity to have someone tell us this, everything was left up to us and we had to find our own way.

The first thing we accomplished was that our son admitted to us that he was taking drugs. This took a long time and we lost a lot of time, since we knew nothing about drugs. I was so afraid of drugs that I did not want to hear anything about them. The two of us spent hours upon hours and even entire nights with our son until we discovered he took drugs. In the beginning, we only noticed that something strange was happening.

We had raised our son so that he would never sit in the bus, but would always offer his seat to an older person; he never passed by an acquaintance without greeting. He is a person with a heart. However, when we started to talk about drugs to others, they thought we were sick because we accused the child of doing something he was not even doing. He was so ready and able to lie—but they are more or less all like that—that he convinced me that he was like we thought he was.

One night, my wife had persuaded me to tell my son that I thought he was taking drugs and I had to gather all my strength, as he was under the influence of drugs at that time. Gordan began to cry hysterically and told me, "Father do you love me at all? The worst thing you can do to me on this earth is to accuse me of being a drug addict. How can you even think that I am like that?!!" I must tell you that he convinced me for the umpteenth time, that he was not an addict. They are ready to do anything! One day, however, there was no way out. We found proof that he was an addict. This was the first victory. But my wife and I were shocked by this experience. As long as we had doubts, we had hoped that it was all not true. At the moment, however, when he admitted it, we believed him. I must tell you that we were ashamed and wanted to keep it a secret. I wanted no one to see it and that it remained between us. These were my thoughts because I knew nothing about drugs. As long as we behaved in this manner, there was no progess in the healing of our son.

Now I know that when you have a son, who is an addict, you need not be ashamed. You have to accept it like any other illness, because, when the addict feels that his parents are ashamed and try to keep it a secret, he will not accept any healing, especially not a community.

After having coped with the fact that our son was a drug addict and had accepted that fact and stopped being ashamed, the situation improved.

Our talk convinced him to let himself be admitted into a hospital in Split. I began to hope that, after several weeks, we would again have a normal son. During the month he spent in the hospital, the doctors convinced me that he was a great guy, that he took nothing, and they asked me why we had brought him to the hospital. I thought I now had a healthy son. I am telling you this so no one can deceive you in a similar situation. They deceived me. The hospital stay brought nothing. You cannot be healed in a couple of weeks or in a few months. In order to be healed of drugs, it takes a long time, much patience and many sacrifices from the parents, as well as from the addict.

The first evening after he left the hospital, he immediately took drugs again. Later he admitted he had taken drugs every day in the hospital. His friends had brought them to him and had handed them to him through the window. They always stick together.

With his coming home, hell also returned. I let him know that I loved him but that I did not want to play a part in his death. An addict in the house dies every day and parents take part in it, even though they don't want to. After a short time, he went back to the hospital, but nothing came of it. So the hospital is not a place that can help addicts.

When my son realized that the hospital could not help him, he decided to join the Croatian Army, not because he loved the army, he could not love it, but because he was under the influence of drugs. He was still taking drugs several times a day. He went into the army to escape from the drugs and his clique and to get out of the city of Split. But unfortunately the drug follows the addict. They exist in every town. He also found the drugs in Pula. From Pula he went into the battle zone, Popovo Polje. Every time he came home, he was under the influence of drugs. Once he did not like what his mother said to him, so she told him that things could not continue like this. He put a bullet in the barrel of the gun, with the intention to kill his mother, me and himself, not because he did not love us, but because he did not know what to do with himself anymore. Only my level-headedness, at that moment, brought him back to reality. I began to laugh. He dropped the gun and left.

He went on the street and was gone for two months. I searched for him every day, although I should not have done that. But I did not know that! One day I met my son; he was carrying a cassette recorder under his arm, which he had taken from a friend in order to sell it so he could buy drugs. It was summer time and he was dirty, neglected and unshaven. I took him home. (I am telling you this so that you see what an addict is able to do!) When I took off his shoes, since he was unable to do so himself, part of his skin came off with his shoes. He had not taken off his clothes and shoes for two whole months. But he stole every day in order to get money for drugs. He was not ashamed at the time. He did not think about it because the heroin impaired his brain.

For these two months, he had to go to prison. My wife and I knew this and even requested it because we knew that any place would be better for him than the street. It is true that his stay in prison brought some positive results, because we could convince him that he needed to go into a community and he agreed. (Because of criminal actions, especially because of the thefts, he could have spent up to three years in prison.)

Now I can say that Sister Elvira lit up hope and a deep conviction in our hearth, that I will have a son again, who I can be proud of. But I will never permit him to repeat again what he did to our family.

We both, have made many mistakes but not because we wanted to make them. Mainly, I was not prepared that my son, at the age of 15, would leave the family he had been dependent on and was attached to, and go on the street, not willing to resist the evil.

In his childhood, he also had several traumas. When he was three years old, we had two possibilities: either to quit working or to send him to kindergarten. Perhaps someone might say that hundreds of children go to kindergarten, and nothing happens to them. That is right, but hundreds of children don't cry each morning when they have to go to kindergarten. Each morning when he said goodbye to his mother, he cried so bitterly as if he would never see her again in his life. A similar situation took place when he began to go to school. Instead of remaining at home to see him off to school and to welcome him back after school, I put the key around his neck and left the seven-year-old child alone in the house to take care of himself. I did this because I wanted to make sure he had everything materially, so he could live well. But now I understand that material goods are not the most important thing in life.

I also understand that I was not patient enough with my son. He showed a great desire to work with me. I was egotistical and never satisfied with what he did. I only noticed what he did badly and never what he did well. This made him sad. Some of my mistakes were due to my upbringing; but I did not get addicted to drugs.

I have to admit one more thing: I did not give my children what they deserved. I did not have them baptized. My son had himself baptized when he was 22 in the Church in Medjugorje and my daughter, when she was 18 years old.

Recently, I was in Italy and my son gave testimony and said that he was hoping for a present from his father. I thought he meant something material, but he continued, "I expect from my parents that they get married in Church." We have not done this until now. But I promise that we will do it.

MAJA BUDIŠA

I am a mother of an addict. My husband talked about our life and the whole tragedy of our addicted son and there is no sense in my repeating everything again. I want to tell you what happened in our family during the last three and half years, since our son has entered into the community and in relation to what went on before he entered the community. While our son Gordan was in prison, we searched and asked everywhere whether there was any hope to save him. While searching, we met a priest and asked for his advice. He referred us to the community of Sister Elvira. Thereafter, we went into the community in Ugljane and Medjugorje. We talked with the young people in the community and realized that our son, Gordan, could be rescued. When we understood what the community was all about, we began to prepare Gordan for this step while he was still in prison. This was not easy.

It took much time, many words and much love to convince him that the community was his only salvation. We brought him information about the community and talked to him about it. We tried not to praise the community too much so that he could form his own opinion when he got to know the community. We directly went to Medjugorje after he left prison. We didn't even go home. I was anxious about how he would bear all this and react to it. After he had spoken personally with the boys in the community, he said to me,"Mother, no problem. I will go in the community." After the difficulties and misery in prison, he thought the community seemed to be the right solution for him. Since the moment of his entry into the community, our life began to change.

You have already heard that my husband and I were not wed in Church. So it is clear that God and faith were not present in our family. I believe that this is one of the reasons why my son fell under the unfluence of drugs. He reproached me many times why we did not have him baptized. He did this himself and he would also like us to get married in the Church. We hope that we will do so at Easter time, 1997 in Medjugorje.

When drugs are present in the family, then one really loses everything. The person no longer knows why he lives and what he lives for. Fear and a horrible uncertainty are always present. I went into his room and was always afraid to find him dead. I would return home from work, and open the door and say, "God, please don't let me find him dead!" When I would find him alive, I immediately would ask myself another burdensome question, "What did he sell from our house today?" I went to work in order to earn a living for him. Dear friends, it is terrible to experience what we have gone through.

I, the mother of an addict, want to say to you, when you have doubts about your child, talk to him, look for advice and help from the community in Medjugorje. Since Gordan is in the community, the most beautiful thing that has happened in our family is that we pray the rosary each day. We go to Holy Mass regularly. We experience a beautiful unity with the parents of other addicts, whose sons are also in the community. We have met so many wonderful people during these last two years! Only the community has brought back strength, love and hope in our life. It is not possible to describe what the community has brought back into our family. Our dead family, in which there had been no laughter, no joy and no true life because drugs had brought death, became a family of joy and peace.

Drugs are terrible. You never know when death will visit you, it can be at any moment. This is a terrible feeling. However, drugs brought faith and prayer into our house. Faith really saved us and resurrected us from the dead. Today, after three and a half years in the community, I am again a happy mother. When I gave birth to him, I was the happiest mother in the world. When he admitted to us that he was taking drugs,

I was the unhappiest mother. I prayed often that he would die, that he would exist no longer, because I was ashamed of everything, because I had no strength to accept this cross— the fact that I had a drug-addicted son. When I realized this was my cross that I have to accept and carry, I saved my son. Believe me, today I am again proud of him. It is not easy to again become a human being after this swamp he had been in. Now I really hope that he will again be a person and to-morrow a good and wonderful father and that he will help many to save themselves also from evil.

VII. WE MET AND FELL IN LOVE

It is surely interesting and helpful to read the testimonies of these young people because Jakov had been in the community, left it and started a family. This testimony is interesting because one often asks what happens to those, who have left the community.

JAKOV ČOTIĆ

My name is Jakov. I am 35 years old and lived almost one third of my life in the world of drugs and evil. I had the wish to change my life, but each attempt was in vain and I became more and more discouraged. But then one day, I heard the words of a small, but great woman, Sister Elvira, who said, ***"Each addict is a wonderful pearl that has fallen into a swamp and it is enough to take it in the hand, to polish it, so that it shines again."*** I understood that not everything was as black as it seemed, that I was worth something and I decided to go into the community in order to change my life. Through my confidence in Sister Elvira, I also regained my own confidence, my belief in God and prayer. I spent four and a half years in the community, during which I got to know the true values of life, which I had forgotten or had never known. After three years in the community, I met a girl, who was looking to save her drug-addicted brother (while I am writing this, he has already been in the community one year!) We befriended each other at various meetings, while her brother was getting ready to enter into the community. Slowly our friendship grew deeper because we had the same outlook on life. She was all I had dreamt about but I thought that this was unattainable for me: a friend, a sister, a brother, a mother and a girlfriend. So I had the wish and felt the need to have my own family and thus also to leave the community. I was aware of the, difficulties and responsibilities awaiting me. I knew that I had to cope with it, as I had been taught in the community. I knew that I had to be honest and sincere, that I had to do without many things and make sacrifices and I also knew that-if I wanted to stand on my own two feet-I would also have to go on my knees and pray to God, for strength, to God, who will never disappoint or abandon me.

After having left the community, I was confronted with the great distrust of the people, who had known me as a bad person. They judged me and pushed me aside. I also was confronted with my family, who did not understand me, who wanted to help me, but did not know how. Somehow it was better that way, because I had to be the one, who fought, who had to find his own way, using what I had learned in the community. My family did not accept the girl, whom I had decided for, which was a further frustration for me.

Irregardless of our surroundings, our relationship grew more stronger and true (and as a result, also I). We concentrated on what was inside of us and did not waste time on exterior looks and above all, we prayed for our relationship. I was confronted with myself and my evil sides, my pride, my selfishness, my wish to show myself different from what I really was, and to be as I was not but wanted to be, and with many other negative charateristics. We wanted to get married, but neither the girl nor I had a job and one cannot live off love and air alone. Two months after leaving the community, I knocked on every door to look for work; but there was no work neither for me nor my girlfriend. But we did not get discouraged. We lived in the hope and believed that it would get better; it was clear to us that there would be temptations and this is why we knew we had to be patient because one cannot have everything all at once. Finally, we decided to get married, regardless of whether we found work or not. Two days after this decision, Snježana got a job and shortly thereafter, I. We were overjoyed and were aware of the divine providence with which the Lord had rewarded our sorrows.

I don't want to conceal that there are difficult moments of nervousness, of conflicting ideas and characters, but I know I must still pray much more and believe in what I have to do and then, I will also be rewarded. We prepared ourselves for the sacrament of matrimony by living the values of premarital moral purity and we are still living it today as a couple because it helps us not to waste time with external things. We feel that our souls, not only our bodies, have become completely one. We believe in the blessing of our togetherness.

While I am writing this, one and a half years have passed since I left the community. I have been married for one year and I visit the community regularly. It is very important for me to meet with those with whom I learned how to live. This refreshes me always and, in this way, I can be thankful for all that I have learned in the community. Now I feel daily how beneficial each moment is that I lived there. I realize that I have not stopped living in the community and it will be all the worse for me, if I stop, because I then would surely not be as content as I am now.

I thank God, Sister Elvira, and the community because they taught me to love selflessly, to forgive and to live, hoping for a better tomorrow, to trust people, to endure sorrows, to give oneself to others and still much more. I am thankful for the gift of my wife, Snježana, and the love that exists between us; I am thankful for the gift of the family, thankful for the strength we receive in order to be able to carry our crosses, thankful for the smile and the joy, which help us on our way.

SNJEŽANA

I am Snježana. I'm a girl that lived in a family, in which everything seemed to be in order. The money (the material aspect) was most important, we adored it. I am a girl, who fulfilled all duties in the family and school, who was an exemplary student and finished her studies. I behaved as a girl should; I was quiet, I strived for joy, mutual love, togetherness and prayer in our home. But all that was missing. One day the small, seemingly present joy of my family was destroyed. We discovered in our family that my younger brother was a heroin addict. My parents knew that my brother was an addict, but for them, work and money were still more important than the health, happiness and salvation of their child. For me, this was very difficult but, at the same time, I decided to help my brother because there is salvation and I wanted to find it. I believed in this salvation. (Today I know that, at that moment, God was with me and He blessed me in my decision). In the beginning, this was my Golgotha; we tried wrong ways, the doctors and psychiatrists tried to help him with tablets. But nothing helped. We decided to go to another country because we thought the change in surroundings would help. We went to far-away Australia and there, something decisive happened. God gave us the grace that we got to know Christian families. In addition, we got to know Sister Marija Ćosić and Father Marijan Glamočki. For the first time we met people, who listened to us, who wanted to help, who gave us love and showed us the right way we should take, and that's the way of Christ. At that time, my brother not only freed himself of drugs but also I felt the love and grace of God. He embraced our souls and healed them. There we received our first Holy Communion and the sacrament of Confirmation. Enriched with the love of God and prayer, we returned full of joy to our family, and wanted to share with them the joy of union with Christ, but were confronted with complete rejection, we were even laughed at with the question, "Where is your God?" These words wounded our hearts and souls deeply, which had just been enriched with the grace of God. Every day they wounded my brother more and more, he felt completely misunderstood by his family and so he fell again into the claws of heroin.

Thank God that He continued to remain with me. He was my strength and my support. 'When my father and mother abandon me, the Lord will accept me.' I listened to His voice within me that said, "Believe, pray, pray . . ." One day my brother, for whom I was a support, a friend, a sister, a mother and a father, told me about the community of Sister Elvira. He told me he could only find salvation there. He told me about the young people, who had been addicts and were now healed. We decided for the community and, while he was preparing to go there, I went with him one day in order to get to know the community.

Early one morning on the way to the community, I was so excited and full of expectation as to what I would see and experience, and I asked him, "Now where is it exactly?" He answered, "You see, in the distance the smoke coming out of the chimney!" While I was looking at the smoke, as it was happily rising to the sky as if it were singing, a picture came into my mind-that of a happy family-and that is how it was. I encountered happy and smiling faces, young boys, who almost exploded with joy. I saw Christ in their eyes, I felt that they wished us well. This was a house, in which one spoke the truth, in which God was praised and loved, in which there were no secrets and no embellishments. I felt that I could say the truth about my brother and talk about the problems within my family and nothing was expected from me in return. At that moment, I realized that this was the salvation for my brother. He went into the community and I decided to remain at his side and to follow his life in the community (also here the Lord played a great part in my decision!).

Then I met Jakiša, a guy, in whom I had confidence from the first day, because I believed that he lived with all the values taught in the community and, above all, he was steadfast in his prayers. I wanted to be a friend to the boys, to give them a helpful hand so that they felt they had support and were not rejected, so they knew they were valuable persons; on the other side, in these discussions, I also found myself, because we were going on the same way, the way of faith, love, truth and life. Life with Christ took over the first place in our hearts.

In the meetings and talks with Jakiša, mutual sympathy developed. However, great difficulties arose. After three months, my brother left the community; but I felt that the community, the boys and Jakiša continued to wish me well and they gave me the strength to remain steadfast and to believe in the community. The sympathy, that had developed between Jakiša and myself, did not stop but, the Lord made it grow even stronger.

It was very difficult to tell the parents (to bring another addict, of course a healed one, into a family that already had an addict among its members, and so did not believe the newcomer and doubted everything he said), the friends and those in the vicinity, that I was in love with a former addict. In the depth of my soul, however, the Lord was guiding me and gave me His helping hand and His comforting words. The wishes of Jakiša and myself were guided by prayer. While I was kneeling in my room and Jakiša was doing so in the chapel of the community, we were united through Christ.

The first person, who blessed my decision to marry Jakiša and who helped me the most, was 'mamma' Elvira, as we two used to call her. She wished for us to get to know each other. While I was talking to Elvira, I felt the rays of a great love for both of us in her eyes. She looked at me with tenderness and love and so lovingly, that, still today, her gaze is constantly with me. Her words were decisive for me when I talked to her about all the problems that were going to confront me: the condemnations, the non-acceptance by the parents and the surroundings, my fear that I would hurt and wound the hearts of my parents.

She looked at me with eyes full of joy and said, "Snježana, if I had to choose a husband, then it would be Jakiša." She got up, embraced him, kissed him, pressed him to her heart and, at that moment, my heart also said: YES.

YES-to my happiness, to the great love we have for each other.

YES-to believe in the community, to live the life of the community.

YES-to the salvation of my brother, who again returned to the community and, thank God, has already been there for an entire year.

YES-to give yourself and to show the right way to all young people, who find themselves without a goal in life, in the darkness of drugs and alcohol.

I could still say many times YES, but I know only one thing for certain, that I have to praise God and thank Him for the gift of the community; but most of all, my great, great thanks goes to 'mamma' Elvira, who loves the lost hearts and souls.

We have now been married for one year. It is a marriage, which has been built on the pillars of Christianity, a marriage which we try to live after the example of the Holy Family. The fundamental thing that makes us happy and content is the steadfastness in prayer and the faith in Christ. Our marriage, as any other, experiences sacrifices, renunciation, sorrow and devotion, but all these are also stimuli of a life together.

VIII. ORA ET LABORA

God, the Creator of the whole world, believed man capable to work in this world and that through his work, he would be able to develop himself and the world. Man is the only living creature that was given an intellect and a free will. God wanted him to be His collaborator. And so one can actually say that man comes into being through work, but not how various philosophies explain that man originated through work. God gave man the talents and, by working, man develops and perfects them.

In his freedom, man can say NO, he can reject his collaborating with God and so hinder his growth and development and thus, will not succeed in his life. He will even be dangerous to himself and his surroundings. Each talent, which is not positively developed becomes the source of evil and bad attitudes towards onself, other people, towards the world and towards God. Only man can stop his growth and so endanger himself.

It is no coincidence that slouth is one of the seven main sins. When one speaks of slouth, surely one does not think of single actions or tasks that a child once neglected to do because he was lazy, but it is a much deeper reality. Slouth is the rejection of and non-collaboration with God, the Creator, which becomes the basis for all other evils. It comes from pride when a person takes his life into his own hands, by rejecting the rules of life and growth, which God, the Creator, has put into the human heart.

The entire nature and everything else was created in order to 'obey' God and man and so human work is assured of its success. 'Obedience' of nature and its laws is the basis of technology and all inventions.

What would happen if a seed, which is cast upon the earth would say, "I don't want to grow!" or a physical law would say, "I don't want to cooperate?" Then no technological development would be possible.

A man, who does not work, will become spiritually and mentally ill and is open to destroy himself.

Next to work, which is the creative activitiy of man, there is also another dimension and that is prayer. Prayer is a contact with God, the Creator. It is exactly here that man differs from the animal world because he needs the spiritual contact with God. Without this contact, man becomes a wanderer in this world, without a goal and becomes a slave of himself, of nature and of material things. When a man lowers himself onto the materialistic level, he becomes more dangerous than any animal. From the behavior of animals we know that no animal eats or drinks more than it needs. Even the most bloodthirsty animal is not dangerous to his surroundings, once he has satisfied his need for food and hunger.

Only man becomes insatiable, aggressive and destructive when he is spiritually hungry and empty.

Here there is an opportunity for drugs, alcohol and all other evil vices. Man cannot bear and tolerate spiritual emptiness and that is why he has to replace it with material and physical pleasures, even if it means self-destruction. A man, who is spiritually fulfilled, cannot fall into addiction because God gives freedom and fills the heart. After much searching and wandering around, St. Augustine explained this with the following words, "God, you have created our heart for you and it will not rest until it finds rest in you."

Although one says the rule 'pray and work' is a Benedictine rule, it is really a general rule for everyone. The person, who prays and works, who with his spirit has contact with God, the Creator, and who, with his talents collaborates with God, remains free and spiritually and mentally healthy (therefore, also work is a contact with God and a form of prayer!)

When man is bound, in this case by drugs or other addictions, the only true medicine to find the balance of your relationship with God is through prayer and work.

In all the testimonies of the young people, one clearly sees that healing starts at the very moment when they accept work and prayer. Generally, this creates opposition because the gift of work and the spiritual life have usually been destroyed. As long as 'work and prayer' has not been accepted, life in the community is a real torture and sorrow. This is why the young addicts find it so hard to decide to enter into the community and are usually 'forced' into the community by the terrible choice between jail or the eventual death through an overdose. The fear of death and not the love for life are decisive in these difficult moments but, in itself, this surely is not bad.

It is also not strange that many young people have admitted in their testimonies that they had much of everything that their parents had given them everything and, in this affluence, they reject every collaboration with God because it means growth and it is not always pleasant to grow. Then they open themselves to the addictions, which enslave and deaden them, and so reject the gifts they have been given and distance themselves from God and others.

When a person is healed so that he can collaborate with God and he begins to work and to pray, he becomes a happy person. Here again a space opens up for much hope: persons, who had been destroyed and had raised a cup of poison to their lips, become true collaborators of God through work and prayer, when they wake up from their apathy and fascination. They bring hope and peace back into their families and create happy new families.

THE VALUE OF LIFE

Sister Elvira repeats often that one does not heal young people from drugs or alcohol but that the sense for life is being healed. When one discovers the sense for life and begins to love life as a gift, then one will also protect it.

The greatest sickness of today is that one does not recognize the true worth of human life.

The child begins to lose the values of life when his parents are more concerned about his or their material needs than the spiritual ones; for example, when they stop to enjoy life and only find pleasure in things and success in their work.

Already from the moment, when a mother is told that in her womb, the miracle of the creation of a new life took place, her first reactions are decisive for the child and for his entire life. When the mother and the father are happy about the child, a positive relationship is formed throughout his life. However, if he is being rejected, the child may have problems during his entire life, especially as far as the meaning and value of his life is concerned. The formula is very simple: if no one is happy about me, when I am not important to anyone, how can I be important to myself!!

How often do parents say that they gave their child everything, that they did everything for their child and cannot understand why he fell into drugs. They must then sincerely ask themselves, if they had forgotten about the child himself, while only working for him and his material needs.

Maybe we can explain this in a short and touching story.

A small son asked his father why he never stayed with the family on Saturday and Sunday evening. The father answered that, aside from his normal work during the week, he had to have a second job on Saturdays and Sundays, in order to earn enough so that the family would have everything. The son accepted this answer quietly, without asking another question.

On a Friday evening, the son asked the father again if he would also go to work the next day. The father said yes. The son asked, "And how much do you want to earn for us tomorrow?" When the father said the likely sum, the son simply suggested, "Stay with us, I will give you that amount because my aunt recently gave me so much money."

The child needs the presence of the father and mother, he should be with them, play and talk with them. How many young people complain that they were left alone so often. And this loneliness forces them into the cliques, which accept them, and when the cliques are bad, everything goes wrong.

To enjoy life means to help people, to realize that one's life is valuable and that it has a meaning also if one possesses no material goods, also if one is small or old, healthy or ill.

In today's world, life has become terminally ill. How many small children are being killed because one calculates and counts how much their livelihood will cost and one comes to the conclusion that it is too expensive? That is why, the elderly and sick are no longer safe because for them-only in another manner-their lives are at stake.

Life can only be healed through Him, who has created it and only through those He has created. This is why it is important to find a group of persons and also individuals, who will accept these terminally-ill people unconditionally.

We, who know God, our Creator, who delights in each one of us, who loves us, who wanted us and who knew us before our parents did, have an opportunity to be healed during our life, even if we have been rejected and wounded by the others.

The truth we heard about Jesus, "You are my beloved Son", applies to every life and here begins our healing. Nevertheless, there must be one person among us, who tells this to people.

This is the strength of the communtiy of Sister Elvira. There is togetherness, love, mutual acceptance, help, patience, but also communal prayer and common work.

From the testimonies of the young people, we can see the following: the first thing they notice is that someone is pleased with them, the community is pleased with them and the guys in the community are pleased with them. Someone, who has lived through drugs and its consequences, knows well that he is being rejected by all and is dangerous for others, that no one is pleased with him and that everyone is afraid of him. This is actually a condition of hell.

So the new experience, that someone is pleased with him, turns out to be the beginning of the new life.

Then they begin to enjoy their own life and the first signs of trust in the community when they become the 'guardian angel' and are being entrusted with the care of a new person, who comes from the same world and with the same problems as he. By serving the other, they start to enjoy their own life and are satisfied by the gift of serving others.

Logically, then follows the pleasure of belonging to a community and a family, then forgiving and reconciliation come about in the family, inner healing comes about and conditions are created so that life can begin outside of the community.

In spite of all the conditions, human life has a meaning when the individual person discovers God because God gives him meaning. The basic question in the catechism is, "Why is man on earth?" The answer to this question is, "Man is on earth to know God, to love Him and to serve Him and come happily into heaven." Nothing else can satisfy the human heart and any other action mortally wounds man and kills him.

It is a great grace and condition for life to discover the value of life and so to remain healthy in soul and body and to be able to heal others.

THE TYPES OF DRUGS

In any case, I also wanted to write a short chapter about drugs. Usually one speaks about light and hard, natural and synthetic drugs. After a talk with Sister Elvira, I realized, that this was not only unnecessary, but even dangerous. All drugs are the same. The person, who begins to take drugs, takes what he thinks will help him to escape from his reality. At the beginning, he takes just so much of a type of drug as he needs to escape from his reality and to overcome it. When he returns to reality and faces it, he has the wish to run away again. For this new escape, he needs stronger doses in order to get away from his reality. A stronger dose distances the addict still further from reality, dazing him in an even more fascinating way; this is why, after he comes off the drug, he falls into an even deeper reality that he cannot bear. For the renewed escape from reality, he needs an even stronger dose and so a devilish circle is formed, from which it is very difficult to come out of and escape from.

All types of drugs cause two types of addictions: physical and mental ones. It is much easier to free and cleanse oneself physically than mentally because, in the beginning, the problem of drugs is never physical, but spiritual-mental. But drugs destroy the spirit, the soul and the body. Only love for oneself and the others can rescue a person from this evil.

THE CONSEQUENCES OF ADDICTION

The consequences of addiction from drugs or alcohol generally cannot be foreseen by the individual, the family and the community.

Dependency leaves terrible trails on all levels, that is in the soul, in the spirit and in the body. When one compares this with a physical or mental illness, only then can one grasp the entire tragedy of addiction. A physically-ill person can be-and often is-a respected person, a true blessing for his family. A sick child is, in most cases, the child, who is closest to his parents and returns the love most strongly. Someone, who has been ill since birth or is mentally ill due to his environment, is surely a heavy cross, but is still bearable. He is dependent on the help of others, he lives his entire life in his own world and, while the others are helping him and taking care of him, they themselves, develop mentally and spiritually. In families, in which there is a physically-or mentally-ill person, there is always a solemn atmosphere of peace and devotion, of deep understanding for each other and a readiness to help each other.

I recall the thoughts of a mother, who had four small children and whose husband was a chronic alcoholic, who, in his drunkeness, was very violent towards her and the children. The family was full of fear and mistrust, which left deep scars in the physical and mental development of the children. She was very depressed and bitter about the situation in the family and said, "Why this cross? Would he or I be ill, we would take care of one another, help each other, we would be happy and the children would be satisfied. But so, this unnecessary cross destroys us spiritually, and we become totally poor!" It is true, the children of alcoholics are very often reserved, fearful, have difficulties in learning, cannot concentrate and can spend their entire lives in fear, without happiness and peace. The family of an alcoholic is also being destroyed materially.

When a guy or girl take the path of drugs or alcohol, they first hide this for some time, they begin to lie and to steal. In such a situation, they lose the correct feeling for the value of life, in general, they use all their spiritual, mental and physical strength to obtain the narcotics. The moment the family discovers this, tragedies, quarrels, conflicts, hatred, mistrust and accusations develop. Disorder and unrest become the daily food of the family. And when such food is needed in a family, the whole family falls apart. The parents accuse each other, one loses joy and peace. And the family without peace, becomes a family without life.

A destroyed individual and his family with him become a cancer in any society. Violence, burglaries and thefts begin, up to the moment when the addict comes into conflict with the police and ends up in prison.

Since addicts are not able to work, earn money, to begin a family and to live in a community, all people are being damaged. Addicts become a great burden for hospitals, social institutions and prisons. Each year the drug destroys hundreds and thousands of individuals and, with them, also their families, which is very costly for society, as it has to care for the addict.

While the Biblical meaning of peace is the spiritual, mental and physical good of an individual, the family and society, drugs are an actual satanic attack on all these levels of a human being. It also attacks the family and society on all levels and destroys them continuously.

Here it is only right to ask the question, why the families and the entire society cannot find ways to break through this deadly chain of drugs. Why does life not defend itself against this death and why does it not stop it? Why does the motherly love, which, according to its being, is love, that serves life, not have enough strength and courage to seriously stand up against this deathly wave of the consequences of drugs?

On one side, it is a spiritual problem. He, who believes will neither really destroy his own life nor that of the others, but will serve life. Drugs enslave the individual and, through him, they enslave everything surrounding him.

The problem also lies in the generally accepted outlook on life. If we do not defend each life with the same courage

132

and decisiveness, it is a sign that the spirit of destruction of life has crept into the world and so it seems, at the moment, that the deathly claws of drugs are stronger than the saving force of the love for life. The problem of money is strongly connected with this. Many people become slaves of money. Money is their Lord and God and they do everything for it. What and how they work is not important to them at all. They use all possible means to obtain it. This is why they are not afraid to sell drugs for a lot of money, to distribute them, and to force the miserable addicts to steal and be violent in order to obtain money to buy drugs; so, drugs become a very profitable business.

Although this is one of the most brutal and inhuman businesses, there are people in every nation who sell drugs, and, with new addicts, they keep enlarging their circle of customers.

Why doesn't the government and its security organizations get involved more often in the actions against drugs? Often we accuse presisely those responsible in government that they are involved in drug affairs and, while filling their own pockets, they are killing the young people. Each penny they receive in this manner, becomes blood money, which they earn from these young victims.

Some individuals and the responsible levels of society become grave-diggers of their own people, just in order to obtain money. It is clear that there exists an entire organization for the distribution of drugs, which an individual cannot infiltrate, but if he dares to oppose them, then he often is physically harmed.

Unfortunately, the Church does not do much against this evil, as if She had lost this profound motherly instinct to protect and defend every life.

Sister Elvira and the others, who want to save young lives, are, however, evidence that the spirit of God stimulates indi-

133

viduals to serve life. From the history of such efforts, we see that these people often remain lonely, that they are not being supported and helped but that even difficulties and obstacles are put in their way.

Mary is the Mother of all living and in Her school of peace, the gifts must be developed, with which one protects life and rescues it from the claws of death.

THE MECHANICS OF THE ADDICTION CYCLE

According to his nature, man is an 'addict'. No one can live for himself, one is dependent upon the other and depends on him, as well as on material things. No one can free himself entirely from air, food, water, from the laws of nature, life and death. God has so created the world and the world can only exist like this. Man is an 'addict' because he needs love, friendship, the mother, the father and the friend. It only depends upon the way a person develops himself and how he grows, what the others do with him, what he does with people and what he does with things. He can develop positively, as God had wished from the beginning, and reign over nature in friendship with God and mankind; but he also can become a slave, addicted to people and things. This is why each person has to make decisions in his life, which place him on one side or the other. And here, he is dependent upon the others. If he is together with good, free and honest people, it will be easier for him to choose the path of love, freedom, honesty and peace; but if he is on the other side, then he falls more easily into slavery and loses his dignity. In neither case must he become like the others and do what the others want. He can make the decision.

Since every person is 'wounded' in his innermost being, the wound can easily be poisoned and the continuation of the poisoning has its laws, just as the healing also has its laws.

In the book entitled, 'Love is the Choice' by Dr. Robert Hemfelt, Dr. Frank Minirth and Dr. Paul Meier, published in Nashville, USA, 1989, the cycle of addiction, which I am using here, is graphically illustrated in order to show the negative mechanics of the cycle of addiction.

Every 'addict' has his 'reasons' and what is shown here explains the disastrous course of addiction in general.

1. At the beginning appears some type of pain, a desire for love and to be loved, a lack of self-acceptance, guilt complexes, various coercions of life or a senselessness of life and boredom.

2. In such a situation, phase 2 begins to develop slowly. The person searches for a temporary escape from the negative feelings and takes what is being offered to him, drugs, alcohol, etc.

3. When he begins to take sedatives, he experiences a relief and liberation and starts to take more and more sedatives, to take them more regularly and so the need arises to take ever increasing doses.

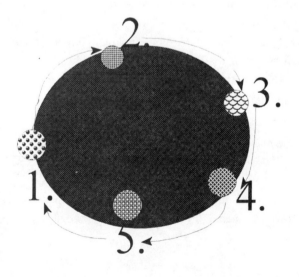

4. In regularly taking higher doses, the consequences appear: loss of health, loss of work, depression, nervousness, feelings of guilt and problems within the family.

5. In such a situation, feelings of guilt and shame again develop, one begins again from the beginning and this continues without end. The healing has become the cause and the cycle has taken on its own dynamic.

So the addiction forms a circle. The remedy one takes begins to direct the person. The body becomes addicted to it. The body develops also resistance and, in order to combat it, one has to take more in order to reach the same effects. Therefore, the use of drugs, alcohol and other means must be continuously increased. For example, heroin is active for approximatley 4 hours in the body, it hightens the sensations, but then ceases to have any effect, so that the person reverts into an even worse condition than before.

So physical and mental addiction develops.

In order for the healing process and the recovery to begin, one needs to know the mechanics of addiction and how to break the cycle. One should, therefore, be aware of the physical and mental addiction. It is more difficult to understand the mechanics of mental addiction than those of physical addiction and to break the cycle.

Sister Elvira always points out that it is necessary to 'throw' the addict out of the house, to leave him on the street without the necessities of life so that he 'knocks his head against the wall', because this is the only way one can get into the circle of addiction and for the addict to accept help.

Through work and prayer one tries to heal the meaning of life and so one is able to enter into the psychological addiction.

This process of liberation is very slow, especially on this level. From everything that happens in the community, one thing is certain-one must do many things and this is why you have to be tireless.

HOW TO RECOGNIZE AN ADDICT

In medicine, there is a very important basic rule: resist at the beginning because the medicine is prepared late. This is true for any illness: the earlier you recognize it, the easier it will be healed. This is also true with dependencies and addicts. It is not so important why someone begins to take drugs or other narcotics, but it is important to recognize it in time and to react in the right way. This is especially true for families and parents. But the parents are very often so involved with their own problems, their work, money and their own plans, that they rarely see their children and have no time for them. Everyone, who begins to take drugs, is caught up in the spirit of lies and untruthfulness and does everything to hinder the parents to look into his eyes, so that, when the parents begin to recognize or suspect something, the addicts will defend themselves with clever lies.

The problem also is that the parents always wish the best for their children and this makes them blind in specific situations. To recognize one's own child as a drug addict, brings deep disappointment and sorrow about oneself and the child. In order to avoid this disappointment, many parents stick their heads into the sand, like an ostrich, because they do not want to see the truth and do not want to be confronted with it. This continues up to the moment when the drug addict causes conflicts in the neighborhood, because of his behavior and, because of thefts and violence, begins to have problems with the police. This is why it is recommended that all parents should be attentive, which only results from living together, meeting one another, talking and spending time with each other. But there are signs, which can be easily recognized and which all addicts have in common.

When a young person starts taking drugs, he becomes very tired, nervous, he comes home late, gets up late, is impatient and aggressive, does not want to work and study, and changes his friends. His eyes are often blood-shot, he continually sniffs (the one who takes cocaine), he has no appetite and rapidly loses weight.

Since he needs much money, he begins to steal in the family. This is why, when one notices things missing from the house, one should be extremely suspicious of one's own child and not accuse anyone else first. The addict loses his relationship to other family members and all respect for his parents.

If and when one recognizes some of these signs and begins to talk with the person involved and takes the right steps, one can help much. One has to control the addict more to help him free himself from his new friends. But one must be particularly careful not to believe his promises.

Parents usually cannot follow these recommendations because they are too busy. But it would be most important that the family changes its way of living, that it maintains togetherness and mutual trust.

Those, who are religious and were raised in the faith, are invited to prayer and true conversion. The addiction begins long before one starts to take drugs. The underlying problem is always the relationship with the parents. When the parents live a disorderly life, one can hardly expect the child to lead an orderly life. A healthy family atmosphere is the best guarantee for a child to grow and develop well; but, the family, in which there is no truth, no honesty, no love, that seems to be perfect to the outside world, creates instability in a person and furthers addiction. The non-acceptance of a child, the rejection of his gifts and successes, make the child open to false friends and groups, which offer him solutions for his state of mind. A person, who has peace in his heart and feels accepted, will not be open to such offers.

Naturally, false prophets, who promise joy and peace, contentment and happiness without conversion, without removing the consequences of sin and disorder are usually the problem. Accusations achieve nothing, they only worsen everything.

IX. THE HISTORY OF THE COMMUNITY

The history of the community began in the heart of Sister Elvira. It began when she, as the fourth of seven children, left her house to search for her father, who was a victim of alcoholism, and to follow the call of the neighbors to bring the father back home. Sister Elvira admits herself, that it was difficult for her and that she was ashamed of her father. But when she followed the call of her spiritual vocation, she was able to forgive her father. The forgiveness healed the wounds in her heart and there, where the wound had been, love and care for the suffering people developed. This love opened her eyes for the youths on the street, who were exposed to destruction and ruin. She could not bear to see such helpless young people, condemned to death and abandoned by everyone. She was not the only one, who had heard the word of God, that Jesus would reward those, who recognize Him in the poor and rejected. She was not the only one of the sisters, who followed the rules of the community and who had the word 'caritas'-the effective love-as part of its name. She was not the only one, who went through the streets of Saluzzo and other towns, and saw human beings destroyed by the consequences of drugs and alcohol. She was not the only one, all sisters had seen this, but none had realized it. She was not the only one in the community, who had made her fourth vow, to serve the poor. Every sister had done that. But Elvira saw the modern poor and recognized Jesus in them. She recognized Him and her heart burned when she met them. She decided to help them and asked the community for permission to do this. The community made Sister Elvira wait a long time for the answer and that meant NO, until she said that she could not take on this new task of helping the addicts. The other sisters had tried to persuade her that she was not able to do this, because she lacked the qualifications. Finally, Sister Elvira left the community in which she had been happy. She left, in order to follow the cries of those rejected ones in the streets. With much suffering and in the light of faith, which also put her on the street, she was looking for them in the darkness. She answered this new call with trust and felt in her own body what her poor, whom she loved, were experiencing. To gather the young people, to pull them out of the abyss, in which the drugs had thrown them, and to prove that Jesus loves them is a true adventure, that only the love can risk that is madly in love with the beloved one.

Love, however, is courageous and inventive.

There is a love, which reflects, a love, which feels, but there is also a motherly love, which exists somewhere in the center of life, which sees the needs of others better and decides to help. This is the motherly love, which urges the mother to jump into the water or fire in order to save her child while at the same time endangering her own life.

While the head of the community only loved in thought and feeling, Sister Elvira was urged by her motherly love, which completely sacrifices itself, to go to the lost sons because she could find no peace until she had found them, as the Biblical Rachel. She found them and for thousands of youths she became a mother, a sister, a friend and a physician. In the 14 years of their existence and activity, she built with them many communities in many countries and on various continents. While working and praying with the addicts, she snatches them out of the deathly jaws of drugs and other modern evils. With them, she is presently building the 'Village of Peace' in Italy so that, when they leave, they will be able to remain close to each other, help each other and to live with each other so that together, they can resist evil.

Inspired by the motherly love, which defends life, Sister Elvira has also already opened communities for girls, she gathers new experiences, she sees the newborn persons and rejoices immensely over each victory of life over death, each victory of love over hate and each victory of freedom over slavery. As long as the present time is being inspired by motherly love, so long will Sister Elvira's community exist. As the flame of the candle radiates warmth and enkindles new candles, so Sister Elvira's courage, which is born in love, enkindles new hearts and radiates pleasant warmth and, with its fire, melts the chains, which are closing many hearts.

This light first spread over Italy and then to Croatia, France, America and Austria and is being enkindled in many other countries.

THE COMMUNITIES IN THE WORLD

The community 'Cenacolo' in Saluzzo is registered as the Association of St. Lawrence. Its aim is to help young people, who have problems, especially problems with drugs, on a moral and social level and to point out their problems in today's society.

The first goal of the community is not work itself, but through work, people are being enabled to serve others with the greatest love.

The community represents a concrete proposal for a way of life, which is aimed at the discovery of the fundamental values, such as the acceptance of, and sharing in the sufferings of others and the experience of Christian life.

From day to day, the number of young people increases, who face the problem of loneliness, while searching for the sense of life and the proper place in society.

The community was founded in July 1983. The central house is in Saluzzo.

Presently, the community takes care of about 600 youths, who live in 23 communities.

1. The Community 'Cenacolo' - Saluzzo - Cuneo
2. 'Letizia' ('Happiness') - Savigliano
3. 'Paradiso' ('Paradise') - Castelmonte, Torino
4. 'Gioia' ('Joy') - Borgaro Torinese
5. 'Speranza' ('Hope') - Envie
6. 'Betlemme' ('Bethlehem') - Borgo san Dalmazzo
7. 'Maria' - Spinetta - Cuneo - for girls
8. 'Regina della Pace' ('Queen of Peace') - Cherasco
9. 'Oasi di San Francesco' ('Oasis of St. Francis') - Rosignano Marittimo - Vada
10. 'Madonna della Neve' ('Our Lady of the Snow') - Bagnolo - Piemonte
11. 'San Giuseppe' ('St. Joseph') - Giustenice - Pietra Ligure
12. 'Santa Bernadette' ('St. Bernadette') - Ade - Lourdes, France
13. 'Scuola di Maria' ('School of Mary') - Mariotto - Bitonto
14. 'Campo della vita' ('Field of Life') - Medjugorje, BiH
15. 'Madonna della Salute' ('Our Lady of Good Health') - Ugljane - Split, Croatia
16. 'Nostra Signora della Speranza' ('Our Lady of Hope') - Florida, USA
17. 'Sacra famiglia' ('Holy Family') - Marene - for girls
18. 'Emaus' ('Emmaus') - S. Stefano Gelbo, Cuneo
19. 'Regina pacis' ('Queen of Peace') - Brazil
20. 'Mariotto' - Bitonto - Bari
21. 'Sv. Josip Radnik' ('St. Joseph, the Worker') - Varaždin, Croatia
22. 'Die Muttergottes der Hoffnung' ('Our Lady of Hope') - Mattersburg - Austria

23. 'Villaggio della Pace' ('The Village of Peace') - Saluzzo - Italy

'The Village of Peace' is a village, which is being built by those who have left the community so that they can remain close to each other... The communities offer all young people, who have problems with drugs and are looking for help, a possibility to stay at no cost and no expense and without conditions. They also accept adults and minors.

Since 1994, girls are also being accepted (particularly wives, fiancées and relatives of addicts). The first houses for girls were built in Spinetta and Marene.

The youths stay at least three years in the community. During this time, they are being helped to become aware of their problems, but also of their possibilities and to realize the value of work, honesty and to discover the meaning of responsibility. For the addicts, work is a therapy, which occupies the will and fantasy, which have been destroyed by drugs.

According to their gifts, the following possibilities for work are at the disposal of the youths: agriculture, carpentry for the needs of the community, facilities to print books, periodicals, brochures, the magazine 'Risurrezione' (Resurrection), the making of furniture, a laboratory to produce icons and other arts and crafts, a bakery, a laundry room, a kitchen, and livestock.

The community receives no support from public institutions. This is its own choice. It lives from its own work and is completely independent. Everything is left to divine providence, which guides those persons who sympathize with the problems of young people.

The life style of the community is like that of a family, where one tries to develop every youth into a strong person, who is free of any addiction. The main goals of their education are:

145

to respect life in all its forms, to share the sense of togetherness, the meaning of interpersonal relationships, the will for
life, the belief in one's own future, talks, reconciliation and
the ability to share everything one has and one experiences
with others.

The atmosphere of friendship, the mutual respect and the
shared poverty, which one lives in the group, makes it easier
for the youths to feel accepted and helps them to come to
terms with aspects of life, which are not particularly interesting.

THE COMMUNITY IN MEDJUGORJE - BIJAKOVIĆI

The community in Medjugorje (Bijakovići) was founded
when Sister Elvira came to Medjugorje for the first time in 1985.
Slowly the concept developed to start a community here. The
land was bought. Many people were afraid to have such a
community in their vicinity because they had no clear idea
about the work of the community. The construction was started
in 1990 on stony ground between Podbrdo and Križevac. Now
there are two complexes, an old and a new one. All houses,
as well as the chapel and the entire courtyard, are made out of
stone and were built with much work by the boys who live
there.

They surely have created one of the most beautiful cor-
ners in that neighborhood and it serves as an example how
one should really build, in order to remain in harmony with
nature.

As they were building a home and everything needed to
live with their own hands, they were, at the same time, devel-
oping as human beings. While working patiently each day on
the hard stone, they were, at the same time, working on themselves.

They are being visited by many pilgrims, who enjoy listening to their testimonies; so, in its own way, the community has become a great witness of recovery and has become a calling for everyone to become aware of the dangers of drugs, but also of the possibilities for healing.

At the moment, there are more than 70 boys in the community. The nationalities and countries from which they come show the power and range of the testimonies of the boys. There are youths from 18 nations: Italians, Croatians, English, Irish, French, Belgians, Swiss, Czechs, Romanians, Americans, Mexicans, Brazilians, Slovaks, Slovenians, Hungarians, Austrians and Polish.

At present, there are about 100 boys and girls from Croatia in the various communities to be healed from their addiction and more and more are coming.

The collaboration between the community and the parish of Medjugorje is very good, especially on the spiritual level: on Saturdays, the community sings during Adoration; at the beginning of August 1996/97, they participated in the International Youth Festivals with very instructive dramas (in 1996 with the play-'From Darkness to Light' and 1997 with 'The Prodical Son') and they assist the parish in various activities whenever necessary. In several cases, the boys help out poor families.

They are often invited to schools and other meetings in order to give testimony.

As far as the parish is concerned, a priest celebrates Holy Mass at least three times a week with them and the priests are at their disposal for confession.

As far as the activities in the community is concerned, they have their own bakery and workshop, in which they make crosses, pictures and other religious articles; they are especially diligent in painting icons.

The daily routine is as follows:

On working days, they get up about 6 am in the morning. Then follows the morning prayer with Holy Mass or, when there is no Holy Mass and when the weather permits, they climb up Apparition Hill. After breakfast, they work until noon. Work is being organized according to the daily needs. After lunch, there is a short resting period. Then the rosary is prayed, followed by more work. In the evening, they pray the rosary, read the word of God and talk about the day, which is the so-called 'condivision' (group therapy); the revision takes place every 15 days.

There is a possibility for Adoration during the night in the chapel and on Saturdays they take part in evening Adoration in the parish church. On Sundays and Feast days, after a certain prayer program and participation in Holy Mass, they play football, weather permitting.

There are always young men, who are preparing themselves to enter into the community. These young men spend the entire day in the community and in the evening they sleep with a local family. These are the so-called colloquials.

CONDIVISION

The latin word 'condividere' means to share something with someone. In the community this specifically means that one often 'shares' personal experiences and life during the day in relation to oneself, the others and work. It really is an exercise to learn to talk about oneself and one's personal relationship to the others. It is a special practice in honesty and truthfulness. To admit in front of others what one has done well, but also not so well, has a positive effect on the one, who talks, as well as the one, who listens.

Each person spontaneously forms an opinion of the other, with whom he lives. The less persons know each other, the further the judgements and opinions are away from the truth; so walls are being built up between people, misunderstandings, condemnations, rejections and wrong judgments are the result.

What did not take place in the family, should take place in this 'condivision'. In the testimony of the addicts, one often hears thet they did not speak with their parents, they had no time for one another and were afraid of each other. So it was possible for untruthfulness to creep in, then a need to lie, to present life and happenings in the wrong light or to completely hide them. When such situations develop in the family or the community, then mutual life and love are endangered and death and hatred, which are destructive and lead astray, also creep in. When a person talks to others about himself, a liberation takes place in his soul, light and peace enter, he frees himself from fear, condemnation and so the path to peace and togetherness is opened. Jesus said that the truth will set us free (cf. John 8,32) and St. Paul said that everything enlightened becomes light (cf. Eph.5,13). This is actually the main therapeutic rule, which has to be accepted in the process of liberation.

Here are some examples of condivision.

The young people talked about themselves and answered the following question:

"Are you content in the community?"

When the answer was YES, one should say why and when the answer was NO, one also should say why.

Following are two testimonies:

1) I am happy with the gift of the community. I would not exchange my life for another. For a long time the friendship with the others kept me in the community. Today it is the beauty of life, which keeps me here. When someone left with

the blessing of the community, I felt something like envy in my heart. I thought, "When will I leave? When is it my turn?"

Now I really enjoy life in the community. I feel like a vital part of the community. I decided to stay in the community. Sometimes I am tempted. Sometimes I am confronted with fears, which take away my peace and joy. I am afraid that I will remain without a girlfriend. Sometimes I think that this life is too hard and I am afraid that I will no longer be able to endure it and many other fears overcome me. This daily life, the friendship of many, the prayer and laughter, free me from my doubts and my fears. I feel completely real. I feel like I have put on the right suit. Each day I have to repeat the decisions and choices, which I am making. Each day is new and different. I often fall and get up again. When I fall, I realize that also others are suffering because of my small problems and my selfishness. I realize that I am poor and inclined to be negative. Life in the community helps me to get to know myself better and accept myself more easily. Often I see immediately when I have made a mistake, but I am not able to correct it. I am not mature enough to admit mistakes and to change them. This is why I often blame the others. When I talk badly and when I condemn, then I am being unjust. But I do the greatest harm to myself.

I have to ask you, Massimo, for forgiveness because I judged you yesterday, while I watched you work. I thought, "Does he still not know how to do this, although he has been in the community for so long?" I am really sorry because I see how hard you are trying and do so much good. I have locked myself in this judgment even though it was not that big. But I really wish all the best for you and I love you. But I suffered more than you because I judged you.

Rafa, I must also ask you to forgive me because I was angry at you. When you read the diary yesterday, you said that we had done bad work. I condemned you by calling you a fool. I am sorry. Had I watched more carefully, I would not have judged that way.

So many times I have also condemned the place Ugljane. I heard about things, which are not good; however, I was able to keep everything to myself and later I was able to talk about it calmly and so I feel more mature. The more I develop, the more I experience. This is really all I have to say.

2. I feel that there are days in the community that I live well and days that I live badly. I have realized that my condition depends on how I live with the others. When I am able to be friends with the others, I feel well. For a long time, I felt that being in the community was not my own choice because I thought that I was forced into it. Now I realize that it is very important to live the values of the community because they will help me in my life tomorrow. I have to learn them in the community. It happens to me that I live badly and this happens each time when I build up a wall between myself and others. When I am proud and nervous, when I am dishonest with the others and when I would rather go to bed than to seek friendship with the others, then these bad things happen.

Today I want to live these values sincerely. Whenever I am content inside, I like the community. Although I am already in the community for four and a half years, I feel like I still need it. It is my goal to always be a friend to the others. I have decided to fight against all my weaknesses and everything negative.

Recently I felt a dislike not only for John Paul but also for the entire community. This happened when John Paul told me to go into another room. I did not understand this, because I thought they did not trust me. I felt rejected, useless and that the whole time I spent in the community had been in vain. But when I talked with John Paul about all this, I understood that it was all for my good. I still feel something in me that keeps me from being completely open and honest. I felt very badly when I told him that I thought he did not trust me. But he convinced me that I should not think like that.

It is the same with you, Rafa. I find it difficult to be your friend. But when we talked about everything, I understood how important this friendship is. I am saying this in front of all of you because I want to feel better. Thank you.

REVISION

The latin word 'revidere' means to see again. According to the program of the community, revision takes place every 15 days. While 'condivision' takes place in front of the entire community, without any comments from those who listen, 'revision' takes place in smaller groups. Also here, each person speaks about himself, the others listen to him, they take part with their thoughts and suggestions and say how they, themselves, experience the person, who is speaking.

This exercise is very important in the process of healing. The others are a help to us in order to understand ourself better. Whatever we do, even if we think that it is only for us and that it concerns no one, it still leaves traces in the hearts of the others. If we are able to talk to another person freely and sincerely and let him know how his words and behavior are affecting us, then we discover a fundamental truth-that each person experiences the other person differently. While we are listening to each other, we get to know ourselves and the others better. We understand and accept each other more easily. We forgive more easily. We reconcile when we see how different we are from one another and how the same word can differently affect the other, depending on them, their mood, and their experiences in their family. Then we become more secure and peaceful.

Here are some examples of revision:

The question for this revision was:

"Why do you remain in the community?"

1. I remain in the community because I need it. I want to break the walls and chains, which hinder me to be free. But what is even more important-I want to be more responsible for myself. I am content because I am not remaining in the community because of a drug problem, since there are also other problems and falls. This week went by well. What I do I try to do well. I work on small things. I am experiencing a successful time. I am happy because I came into the community. I discover more and more how the others are helping me. I try to have a good relationship with all, I try to be open so that I can get to know the others. I want to understand myself better and better. As far as prayer is concerned, I am able to pray better and I can also concentrate better during the day. These are really beautiful moments for me. When it was not easy for me to work, I tried to pull myself together.

If someone would like to say something to help me, I would be very thankful.

Feedback:

- I don't see you very often because you are now working in the kitchen. I see that many come to help you. I think you should have more friendships with younger boys in the community. This is a good way to see how mature we are when we are able to be a good example to the younger ones with our life.

- I also think that it is very important to be with younger guys because you can help them very much, but also, because you can understand better the problems you had before. By being a good example for them, they will begin to come to you for advice, they will be able to develop better at your side and be able to solve their problems more easily.

2. I think this is the right question for me. I don't know why I remain in the community. I am really not here because of my own will. I don't really want to remain here and I also don't want to change. I am mainly here because of the police and the court. Other things don't interest me much. So I really don't have to say much to this question. Concerning last week, I was given other work to do. I was happy about that because I hoped that I would learn something. This gave me the hope to find something positive.

Feedback:

- I see that you have good moments. You joke around with the others, especially the young ones. That is good; but I do think you should change your relationship with the others and start some real friendships.

- I can tell you, it is normal to enter into the community because a certain situation forces you to do so. With 90% of us it was also like that. If you don't open your eyes now and realize that this is a new life, then you will fall back into drugs when you leave the community. Then you will have to again go into a community, maybe not this one, but another. And so it will go on through your entire life. I think that you have to make a sincere entry into the community, if you want to live. Here really life is at stake. I would suggest to you to open your eyes and see things as they should be, look at the other boys, who have changed, and notice positive things.

- I think you should be much happier in doing the things you are doing. You should make sincere friendships with older boys. You must try to be more serious during this time and avoid all superficial things.

THE EDUCATION OF THE PARENTS

In the entire healing process of an individual, the healing of the parents and the family is very important. In order for the parents to be able to follow the healing process of their addicted child in the community, weekly meetings for the parents take place on a regional level. At the moment, these meetings take place in Tugari, Varaždin and Medjugorje. One tries to organize these meetings all at the same time in the various places. At present, this takes place Saturday at 3 pm. One prays the rosary, talks about topics which are important for the parents and one exchanges experiences. In talking to one another, the parents and the others get to know each other better. Prayer is particularly emphasized.

In these groups, one tries to obtain help for the upkeep for the community. However, the purpose of these meetings is more important-and that is, that the parents help each other to grow in their faith and to be healed. Sometimes the young boys come from the community to speak with their parents.

Aside from these regional meetings, the community organizes meetings for all parents on an international level every six months. There the young people, as well as the parents, give their testimonies. These meetings are very useful and helpful for the proper growth of the family and prepare them to receive the healed addict once he leaves the community.

ADDRESSES AND TELEPHONE NUMBERS

1. ASSOCIAZIONE SAN LORENZO - COMUNITA 'CENACOLO'
   VIA SAN LORENZO, 35,
   I - 12037 SALUZZO (CUNEO) - ITALY
   Tel./Fax: (++39) 715-46122

2. "CAMPO DELLA VITA"
   BIJAKOVIĆI
   88266 MEDJUGORJE BIH
   Tel. (++387) 88/651-756

3. "OUR LADY OF HOPE COMMUNITY"
   ST. VINCENT DE PAUL FARM
   5985 S. R. 16
   ST. AUGUSTINE, FLORIDA 32092
   (904) 829 - 6720

X. SISTER ELVIRA EXPLAINS HOW A FAMILY SHOULD BE

Much has been said about drug addicts and we have listened to their testimonies, in which we always heard that the problem of drugs began already long before actually taking the drugs, and that is in the family and in its relationships. I asked Sister Elvira to tell us her ideas about the marriage preparation and about how a marriage should be in order to protect children from addiction.

In her lively and convincing manner, Sister Elvira touched many elements of living together.

Here is what she said:

I think one should put particular emphasis on the personal maturity of two persons, who want to start a family. The most important thing for a young man and a young woman, who wish to get married, is to have the strength to respect one another and the freedom of the other. In addition to the mutual respect, there must be love, the true love for each other so that something positive, beautiful and big can begin.

The problem of drugs and of drug addicts begins already with the question, how and why one gets married and what motivation there is for marriage. Today one hears frequently that people get married in order to somehow put their life in order, to secure their existence, to live somewhere, where they can live independently, to be free and to leave the parents.

These motives are not enough. One must find one's way, but also give structure to one's life, but this is not enough. The motives to start a new family and to give new unique life should go beyond that. No one is like the mother or the father. Although they have given life, each one of us is unique. In the heart, a deep respect should grow for God, the Creator, who never repeats Himself in the creation of a person. Parents always want their son or daughter to be like them.

There are elements (human, religious, emotional, spiritual, psychological and sexual) that are completely different when compared to those of a father and a mother and in this, one recognizes the originality of God. God never repeats Himself and it is difficult for us to accept God, the Creator, who acts so freely. These are the natural conditions, but God has created nature.

That is why two young people, who start the adventure of marriage, must be open for something new, also for the natural and human aspects. I think this is true of any marriage, regardless of religious beliefs.

There are people, among heathens as well as Christians, who are under the influence of drugs. Young people often don't know, which way is correct and true, because parents are no example in their life and are of no support.

Parents must be reliable, sincere, honest and virtuous, they must respect nature, the laws of God and others. Whenever the parents do not believe in God, there exists a law in nature, which is engraved into their hearts. Children have the need for parents to be consistent.

To be addicted means to be dependent upon something, tomorrow, to be dependent on drugs and this starts at the beginning of life. While the child is still in the mother's womb, he lives with everything that the parents live with; he breathes, he listens and he feeds himself with what the parents think and say; the child experiences the reactions, the stress, fear and problems of the parents. If these situations are experienced without hope, and also a person, who does not believe can have hope, then the child experiences fears and hopelessness and is being wounded in his soul.

To hope means to trust that tomorrow everything can change, due to your good will, your logic and your human intelligence. We should not only have Christianity in mind, because then we forget religion and faith are only means, but that the most important things-more than any religion and philosophy of life-are engraved in the human heart. God has created man according to His image and that is why there are divine elements in each person, which enable the person to create true and pure relationships with the others without self-ishness.

After many years of experience in the work with addicts and their families, we try to reach the depth and the heart of the family because the addict is only the branch of the tree, which has taken its nourishment from poisonous soil. A tree consists of roots, the stem and branches. Of five children in the family, one is an addict. We ask ourselves why this is so. One thing is always clear, one has to heal the root: the family.

I am convinced that the parents of the future will be much more conscious and attentive, much freer of any behavior, from which come slavery and dependencies.

Let us remember the situation 25 to 30 years ago. At that time, the terrible chase after consummation, productivity and enrichment began. Everyone ran in order to get rich, to feel well, they wanted to be wealthy, so that they could live without problems and easily obtain a comfortable way of life. They also wanted this for their children. But this was a mistake. Today, we see that this battle for more possessions, for example, a house in the city, a house near the ocean, a house in the mountains and many amenities of life, has really not brought the peace we had hoped for. Many people recognize that this attitude of life is wrong and dangerous. All these conveniences have a negative effect on intelligence, which atrophies; they limit the will and cause the relationships in the family. Today, the son does not need to see his mother, he can put the dirty clothes into the washer himself; he does not need to come and tell her what he wants and needs, he does not have to ask her for anything. Today, there is independence; however, this does not mean autonomy. Autonomy is good because one matures; but independence means that one becomes lonely, isolated and becomes unable to take part in talks and dialogues with oneself, others and God. Many things have made man independent. There are also the talks with the computer, television, the telephone . . .long conversations with people outside the home, which lessen the will, desire and need for dialogues within the home. Formerly, it was not so.

It is clear that one cannot remove the technical possibilities from the house; they are necessary and make things easier. A mother, who has a washing machine, has more time for herself and her family. Through television, we hear what is happening throughout the world, but this should not block what is most important-deepening of family relationships. And this is the most wonderful and helpful thing in the world. If someone has a house, three or four cars, but no one to whom he can talk to in his house, his heart will be poor and will shrink.

How many families have become totally impoverished, as far as their relationships to one another and their conversations are concerned, while becoming materially richer. I am convinced that the families of the future will not let themselves be deceived by these technical things. One does not live well when one has a TV, a radio and a car; but one will try to live a good life with the husband, the children and the elderly. To live well means to use the things technology offers us, but not to forget the soul of the home: which is communication with each other, acceptance of one another, mutual respect, the quest for each other and to live a good life together.

TALK TO YOUR CHILDREN ABOUT YOURSELF

Eighty percent of the young people in the community don't know anything about their father or mother. The parents do not speak about themselves, about their youth, how they got to know each other, how they fell in love and how they fought for one another. The child knows nothing. The parents frequently hide many things instead of telling them to their children.

I recall when my parents told us how they got to know each other; how the parents of my mother were against her marrying my father because he was poor and how they met, in spite of these hinderances. They told us how their parents sent my mother 375 miles away from home so that they would not be able to see each other. They told us how my father went there, and talked to her secretly and how my mother always said that he should leave so that she would not be sent away even further. They often told us this story, while we were sitting at the table.

The young people in the community know nothing about their parents and especially their grandparents; they don't know the history of their family. When a child asks something, he often receives the answer, "What business is it of yours? This does not concern you! You should learn! Do your homework! We work so much so that you can study and finish school, etc. . ."

And so the child's mouth is being shut. This is how one often hides unfaithfulness to one another, premarital relationships, lovers and these are all signs of mistrust towards the child.

True love is open, has no fear and is talked about and so the child feels he is being loved, accepted and wanted. This love is confirmed in the sacrament of marriage. One needs a confirmation of love before God and the world because we are weak, fragile and inconsistent. These are the relationships that help us to remain faithful.

The family assures the child a life in love and peace when the father and the mother harmonize in love and do not deceive the child. This means, again, that they should not measure the education of their child with the mentality of the world, the products of the world, the language of the world and with all the superficial things the world offers. This is a lie. Sooner or later, the child does not want to be a part of such a world, but it does not have the strength to resist. When the parents are honest, they say that their suffering was for their benefit, that it opened their hearts and freed them from some lies and slavery. The parents must not exclude the child from their pain, their suffering and problems in the family. They must let the child participate in everything and hide nothing from him because the child would otherwise feel things and come to his own conclusions. The child will slowly lose his trust when he sees and feels something different than what he is being told.

THE RELATIONSHIP OF THE GRANDPARENTS

In the community we also have families. Very often the grandparents act towards their grandchildren as they had acted toward their own children. For example, a child has a birthday. The grandparents visit their drug-addicted son or daughter in the community, where they live with their grandchild. As soon as the grandmother sees her grandchild, she opens her purse and gives him presents.

When I see that, I react immediately; a few times I even took the parcel or the present and stepped on it with my feet and openly said to the grandparents, "This behavior has destroyed your children and this is why we do not allow you to also destroy your grandchildren. You bring joy to your grandchild because you visit him and spend half a day with him,

play with him, play his children's games with him! Don't give him these false messages, which force the child to love you, because it is superficial and artificial. In this way, the child will always expect a present from you, he will open the purse and will not learn to love; but the heart was created for love. But since you are buying his love with your presents, you show him the wrong way."

THE NOVICIATE FOR MARRIAGE

Recently a family came to visit me. The father was in the community and then the mother also came. Although she did not take drugs, she remained for a year. They were also not married when she came. (We make it possible for the girls to be in the community, so that they learn to live, and this is what we call the 'noviciate' for marriage.) Their child ran towards me and said, "Do you know, Elvira, yesterday I had my ninth birthday!" I asked, "What did your parents give you?" Immediately the child bragged, "My father took one day off,

163

he did not go to work, we took a walk and went hunting." This is important-to have time for the child, to give oneself to him and not only give things and toys.

How many young people tell me that they had lacked nothing, but had no love. This means that the father and mother had no time for the child, did not pay attention to him, did not get to know him and did not notice his reactions. The parents must think about the work that God has entrusted to them. The child does not want parents, who constantly fight and who incessently talk about money and material things. The child wants parents, who play with him, who win and lose and are happy. One has to get to know the child and so hinder him from running away from the family. Then also parents will not treat each child alike because not one child is alike.

How many times have I heard how parents talk about their children and claim that they raised them all in the same manner and do not understand how one of them could have become an addict. But this is exactly where this problem lies!! Children are not alike and, therefore, cannot be treated alike. One has to be with them, know them and raise each child, according to what God has given him. One has to observe them when they play, when they fight, when one forces himself on the other, when they reconcile and when they enjoy themselves. Only in this way can we get to know them.

FATHERHOOD AND MOTHERHOOD - A GIFT IN SERVING LIFE

The father and mother, therefore, have to be aware of the gift they have received as mother and father, of their mission as parents-this great gift. God gives this gift, this charism. In order to do that, one does not need to go to school. They have to have an interest in the family, in being together and in the child; they have to think much more about that than about work or money. Today the families are in danger because they want to program their child too much for school, for sports and music. They are too occupied, trying to make something out of the child, and very often they show their idol as their child, for their own honor. This is a theft and it is not right to have a child to further one's own honor. A person, who does that, is unjust towards the Creator and to the child. But it is a particularly dangerous form of ungodliness when we don't even try to understand what God wishes of the child but only pursue our own wishes.

This is why it would be ideal for the will of the parents and the will of God to be in complete agreement and when the gift of parenthood only serves the development of what God has placed into the heart of the child.

In the community we have young people, who have won many prizes and first places in sports, who became sport champions. But then they reached for drugs because they suddenly realized that their victories, which they had attained with many sacrifices and great efforts, only served for the honor of their parents since, already as children, they had to win and be among the first. But so one does violence to the child; it is an exploitation and instrumentalization of the child, for which one pays dearly, sooner or later, with the destruction of the inner self of the person. One should ask a child if he enjoys doing all this and if he thanks his parents for it.

A CLEAR SCALE OF VALUES

Our main question is, what could we do in order not to be afraid of the future, which might possibly present us with one or two drug addicts? (We, in the community have three addicts from a family with five children.)

The drug will not come into your home, if you are aware of the correct scale of values.

The first value is honesty between you and your wife.

The second value is consistency in your conversations, in the relationships within and outside of the family. You cannot say one thing today and insist on the contrary tomorrow. You cannot be inconsistent. The child realizes if your behavior is not in agreement with what you have said before.

The third value is the spiritual respect of the child. One has to respect him. A child cannot accept nor see the following scenes in a family: quarrels, conflicts, violence and immorality. Parents must respect their child. There are young people in the community, who found pornographic magazines of their fathers when they were eight or nine years old. This has a negative influence on them. They immediately feel when a father has a another woman outside the home. Some youths have told me that they remember, when they were four years old, they went out with their father, who took them to his mistress. Then he told the child to tell the mother that they had been at his aunt and that the father had bought him candy on the way. This is the confusion, which comes into the child and, later, into the adult, and so begins the need for revenge. A child does not say that he wants to take revenge, but he feels it.

One boy told me that, when his father was not at home half an hour later, his mother welcomed a man. They drank coffee, winked at each other with their eyes and then locked themselves into a room.

Many think that a four or five-year-old child does not understand anything. But this is not true. A child understands everything. The child is much more sensitive than we adults because he is much nearer to God; therefore, he is still at the source and takes in everything and suffers much more than we do. Why?? Because we think and try to justify with our logic the things that are bad, wrong and evil.

THE CATHOLIC FAMILY

Everything I have said applies to all people, regardless of their religious beliefs.

But we, Catholics, have an advantage. We must have the courage to meet Jesus Christ. The meeting must be a personal and conscious one.

The young people, who were in the community, often invite me to their weddings; they want my presence. I ask them if they prayed together, if they understood what plan God has for them and if they understood that God wants to create a unique and original family with them, because they are two unique persons. Usually they only smile at me. Once a fiancée looked into my eyes and said, "Elvira, Maurizio knows that I had chosen Jesus before I chose him." And then Maurizio said to me, "Favoleta knows that also I had chosen Jesus before I chose her."

It is well-known, when man is faithful to God then he will also be faithful to people. Faithfulness to God is very important because He did not come to belittle or take away something, but to complete, spread and enrich in order to perfect the love between the two of them. When two young people marry in faithfulness to God and promise this in the name of God in the sacrament of marriage, then they will-before looking at each other-always have the courage to mutually look into the face of Christ and to discuss their problems with Him. If they are in agreement with the will of God,they will surely find the true, just and secure way for the family. In this family, the children and the adults will have the courage to remain and not run away from it. They will live the values, which will make them happy, because the father and mother have lived these values and talked about them. One should talk about honesty, sincerity and truth and teach this to the children and young people. They should instill in them the sense of gratitude; protect them from being enslaved by material things; teach them to share everything with others; and that there are poor people in society, that there are those, who have less than they; teach them that sharing also helps them to be happy and that this happiness enriches them in the world. When a family does not own enough and the parents, because of this, are sad, angry, nervous, ceaselessly driven and full of envy and slander the other, then violence grows within the soul of the child, which is further nourished by their selfishness.

There are enough goods in the world for everyone, the only thing missing is the capacity to share. God thought of every human being, of every child, who is born. Finally Sister Elvira said:

Many are afraid of a drug addict because he is no longer a human being, but a monster. Not only hard drugs, but any type of drug, destroy a person. There are no light or hard drugs. There is something that propels you out of yourself, to lose your mind and once you have lost it, you are ready to do anything. When someone smokes marijuana, he does not think he is smoking something light, but he is only looking for an escape from his situation, he tries to run away from his reality. This is a violent act, which is self-inflicted. If one does this with a knife, a pistol or with something else, is not important. One thing is always the same-the person does something evil to himself. At the moment someone takes the 'lightest drug', he rejects his family, his father, his mother, his wife, his child and everything. This is a violent act. In addition, it is never enough. The organism always needs more. They all started with something 'light'; then the organism needs more, more quickly and more frequently: first, once a day, then twice, then five times a day. In the community, there are young people, who spent up to $700 a day. Then they have to steal. So the drug is, in itself, a negative element. The addict is in an abyss of loneliness. The young people frequently say that the drug was only the last leap into the abyss because they were already lonely, disappointed, empty, fearful and inwardly aggressive; but they could not free themselves from this aggression in any other way. (For example, when the father beats the child because of his nervousness, drunkenness or the like, the wish for revenge accumulates in the child but he cannot show this to his father. So he turns against himself and becomes aggressive!)

A person is not born a drug addict. He becomes one through the process of degeneration of the family and society.

XI. BIBLICAL PEACE AND DRUGS

Let us not forget that God has created man with the deep desire for peace and that he is searching for peace in everything he does. When he loves or hates, when he respects the others or rejects them, when he becomes an addict or frees himself of drugs, when he fights or searches for peace, when he accepts life or renounces it, man is always seeking peace.

The problem lies in the fact that one can search for peace with means, which develop a person or with means that destroy him.

This is why there is a true and a false peace, but also why there are true and false prophets of peace.

The true prophets have always announced peace as a gift of God to man, a gift that destroys sin and destruction through conversion. The true prophets are not afraid to speak the truth and this is why they often died and die rejected and as martyrs.

The false prophets have also announced peace, but they never demand that one leaves evil; they don't talk about sin, but only about the peace that is easily obtained. They have an easier time with people because people are more inclined to believe them and so become their victims. The Biblical peace is an abundance of mental, spiritual and physical goods. However, if only one is missing, then there can be no peace. Only the person, who completely surrenders to God, can have this peace because God is the source of peace.

Drugs, their dealers and users-they are all false prophets - as well as their victims.

Drugs attack and destroy all three human elements: the spirit, soul and body. They are an act against creation, they are the opposite process and a negation of creation.

In its essence, the message of Medjugorje is a call to accept the process of the creation of man, according to the plan of God. This is why one has to fast and pray, confess, take part in Holy Mass, that is, to renew one's entire being in order to have peace.

XII. QUICK ANSWERS TO THREE QUESTIONS

After numerous talks and testimonies, I decided to ask many young people, three short questions, without any preparation and without much time to answer. The questions were:

1. What is the drug?
2. What is the community?
3. Is there any advice?

Elvira:
1. The drug is darkness and disappointment.
2. The community is the place of Resurrection.
3. Dream of great things, of a blue sky, of purity and clear eyes. Look into the mirror. Fall in love with what God has given you-even if you have a crooked nose!

1. The drug is being in the situation, in which I say to every thing: It is all the same to me.
2. The community is life.
3. To decide for the values we have within us!

1. The drug is indifference.
2. The community is a place, in which one frees oneself of indifference.
3. Pray!

1. The drug is Satan.
2. The community is the family.
3. An advice for the family: be careful!

1. The drug is the evil.
2. The community is many persons, who love me.
3. Don't take drugs! You will suffer much!

1. The drug is the last attempt to run away from reality.
2. The community is a meeting with reality.
3. Pray, so that you are not lead into temptation!

1. The drug is the running away from problems.
2. The community is the help on the way.
3. Search for places, where the spirit and the soul are renewed!

1. The drug is disappointment with oneself, the family and society.
2. The community is the solving of my problems.
3. The communication in the family and friendship!

1. The drug is the wrong way to peace.
2. The school of life.
3. Listen and don't burn your fingers!

1. The drug is the running away from reality.
2. The community is living together and understanding and accepting oneself.
3. Enter into a community!

1. The drug is something dangerous.
2. The community is the salvation.
3. If you have problems, come into the community.

1. The drug is a great evil.
2. The community is the help and the liberation from that evil.
3. To listen to the word of God!

1. The drug is death.
2. The community is life.
3. Protect life!

1. The drug is a filthy thing.
2. The community is the way to life.
3. Talk with one another in the family!

1. The drug is the end of a wrong way of living.
2. The community is the beginning of a new life.
3. Be good, so that you will be better!

1. The drug is the evil.
2. The community is the way to a new life.
3. The belief in God!

1. The drug is loneliness.
2. The community is the will to live again.
3. You, who are lonely, come into the community!

1. The drug is a tragedy.
2. The community is life.
3. Life!

1. The drug is loneliness.
2. The community is a large family.
3. Stop the drug! Come into the community!

1. The drug is to be selfish, to be full of oneself.
2. The community is a large family, which helps me not only to free myself of the drug, but teaches me to live.
3. Accept God, life and the salvation!

1. The drug is the wish to have everything.
2. The community is the school, in which one learns to live.
3. Humbleness, goodness and generosity towards the others!

1. The drug is the wrong expectation of a solution.
2. The community is the help.
3. To follow the essential things in life!

1. The drug is the evil.
2. The community is the good.
3. Take no drugs!

1. The drug is Satan. It looks like powder, but behind it is Satan.
2. The community is a great gift from heaven.
3. Life is a serious matter. Don't play with it!

1. The drug is the evil.
2. The community is the help to change what you were not able to change.
3. Try to live by changing the things for the better!

1. The drug is death.
2. The community is life.
3. Look up!

1. The drug is the greatest vice of today.
2. The community is a great gift.
3. For all, who take drugs, there is a place in the community and those, who do not take drugs, should remain free of them!

XIII. THE ROSARY FOR THE AD-
DICTS AND WITH THE ADDICTS

INTRODUCTION

God, my Almighty Creator! You have created me out of love. You have given me life and talents so that I can serve You with them in my brothers in mankind. You have given me the gift of freedom and love. I thank You!

Today I come to You, my Father, through Your Son Jesus, in my name and in the name of all, who have lost the freedom and capacity to love You and the others. I turn to You from my enslavement, in which I have fallen because of drugs. It has taken over my heart, my thoughts and my feelings, it has made me unable to think right and to make the right deci-sions. It has mislead me into evil, into sin, into stealing and into violence. It has distanced me from You and the others.

But I know that You are waiting for me and that You are happy about my return, like the merciful father, who was happy about the return of his lost son.

Send me Your Holy Spirit, so that He prays within me and frees me and gives me the gifts of devotion, strength, wisdom, understanding and love.

Mary, my Mother, I thank You because You were also near me when I was not close to You or my physical mother, and because You will help me to free myself completely and return to the home of my Father.

APOSTLES' CREED

I believe in God, the Father Almighty, the Creator of heaven and earth. I believe in Jesus Christ, His only Son, our Lord; Who was conceived by the power of the Holy Spirit, born of the Virgin Mary, suffered under Pontius Pilate, was crucified, died and was buried. He descended to the dead. On the third day He rose again. He ascended into heaven and is seated at the right hand of God, the Father Almighty, from thence He shall come again to judge the living and the dead. I believe in the Holy Spirit, the Holy Catholic Church, the Communion of Saints, the forgiveness of sins, the resurrection of the body and life everlasting. Amen.

THE JOYFUL MYSTERIES

1. I thank You, O Mary, because You answered to the greeting of the angel: "Here I am, Lord, I am Your handmaid!"

I pray this decade for myself and for all, who are not able to utter words of surrender, because their hearts are no longer free. I also pray for those, who are still free, especially the youth, so that they never fall into the enslavement of drugs, alcohol and other dependencies, and so that everyone can say with You, O Mary, "Here I am Lord, let it be done according to Your will."

Our Father . . 10 Hail Marys . . Glory Be . . .O my Jesus . .

2. I thank You, O Mary, because You visited Your cousin Elizabeth. You helped her and prayed with her. You brought her joy and comfort.

Now I pray this decade for myself and for all young people, who have become addicts and through their behavior, have brought disorder into their families, who have caused their mothers and fathers so much sorrow; for all, who have lost the strength to listen to the elderly because of their inner enslavement.

Come, O Mary, bring Jesus, light and peace into the tormented families and into the hearts of the parents, who because of the problems, in which they were thrown by their addicted children, have lost all strength.

Our Father . . 10 Hail Marys . . Glory Be . . .O my Jesus . .

3. I thank You, O Mary, because You gave birth to Jesus in Bethlehem. I thank You for the joy and love, with which You welcomed Him into Your arms.

With this decade, I want to thank my parents because they gave me life and for everything they have done for me. Since I have been taking drugs, I know that I have destroyed their joy and hope. I know that my mother once said, "I wish to God I had never given birth to you, my son, when you are like this!"

I pray that joy and peace return into the hearts of my parents. I pray for all mothers, who are pregnant today so that they will be able to love their child, protect him, give birth to him in joy and that their children will always be a joy for them.

Our Father . . 10 Hail Marys . . Glory Be . . .O my Jesus . .

4. I thank You, O Mary, because You presented Your Son in the temple. Blessed be the moment when Simeon recognized Him as the Redeemer.

Now I offer those, who seduced me into drugs, all those, who produce and sell drugs and so destroy the others.

May they convert, may they love life more than money and any other pleasures. May they recognize, as Simeon, their light in Your Son, Jesus, and through Him, receive peace. I offer those, who are today in danger of falling into drugs, send them those people, who will stop them and hinder them to fall into evil. May each heart, like that of Simeon, happily await the Lord and recognize Him.

Our Father . . 10 Hail Marys . . Glory Be . . .O my Jesus . .

5. I thank You, O Mary, because You found Your Son, He returned home with You and You raised Him. Your sadness turned into joy.

Today many young people have left their home, they wander the streets of their towns and their sad parents search for them. So many have gone to prison or reform school and their parents can do nothing and are sorrowful and worried.

May each heart of the parents be happy about the return home of their child and may each person, who is in conflict with his parents, happily forgive and accept life in the family. May the families be ready to give their children and young people the spiritual nourishment so that each family can become like Your Holy Family.

Our Father . . 10 Hail Marys . . Glory Be . . .O my Jesus . .

THE SORROWFUL MYSTERIES

Lord Jesus, You gave Your life for us. You died on the Cross with terrible agony. Give me now the grace to be with You, to enter into the mystery of Your suffering and agony, so that I can understand and accept my cross and so that everything is transformed into good in glory of the Father, as also Your suffering and Your Cross were transformed into good and for the glory of the Father. You suffered because You loved, but I suffer because I have no love. You suffered out of Your own free will, but I suffer because I have become a slave. As I trust in Your mercy, I now begin to go with You on the way of Your suffering. Give me the grace to remain with You so that I do not fall asleep, as Your apostles fell asleep in the Garden of Gethsemane, and so that I don't run away, as they scattered.

Send me Your Holy Spirit now, may He lead me in prayer.

Mary, teach me to follow Your Son also in moments of suffering and agony, as You also were next to Him and suffered with Him.

CREED

I believe . . .

1. I thank You, Jesus, for Your suffering in the Garden of Gethsemane, for Your loneliness and Your fear and for having sweated blood. I thank You for the words, "My Father, if it is possible, may this cup pass by Me, but not My will, but Your will be done."

You suffered fear and distress, loneliness and abandonment and You were deeply hurt by the apostles, who fell asleep and by the betrayal of Judas.

I pray this decade for all young people, who have fallen into drugs and other addictions and who suffer terrible agonies. Look at them now and help them to overcome fear, distress, loneliness and everything that addiction causes. Free them of every pain, which is the result of their addiction and of every temptation, into which they have fallen, such as violence, theft, lies, cheating and the lack of will. May they open themselves to the love of the Father and His mercy and stop to betray themselves, their parents and You.

Give them back their peace and the strength to resist all temptations.

Our Father . . 10 Hail Marys . . Glory Be . . .O my Jesus . .

2. They bound You on a pillar in front of Pilate and scourged You. This was a pillar of shame and mockery. You were bound to this pillar. You patiently endured everything.

I now pray to You for all, who are bound through drugs or alcohol, who scourge themselves and kill their human dignity, who have bound themselves, as well as their families, to the pillar of shame, violence and suffering. I offer You all the wounds in their souls, all wounds in the souls of their parents so that You can heal them. Help all families, O Lord, who are being scourged bloodily today because of an addict in their home and give them Your peace.

Our Father . . 10 Hail Marys . . Glory Be . . .O my Jesus . .

3. They wove a crown of thorns for You and pressed it onto Your head. They ridiculed You as king and put a red robe around You to mock You. Many fingers helped to weave Your crown and to press it on Your head. You also endured this patiently, You were humiliated, mocked, spat upon and provocated.

Lord, You know all those, who today are weaving crowns of thorns for young people, because of their desire for money, by supplying them with drugs and seducing them onto the wrong path. How many humiliations and mockeries do the addicts have to endure-You know it.

I ask You, convert those, who weave crowns of thorns, who collaborate with evil and destroy so many lives. Give them the grace to convert and to stop doing evil. Look at the young people who, in their families have been crowned with the thorns of loneliness and so are inclined to become slaves of drugs and alcohol. Free them and give them back their human dignity!

Our Father . . 10 Hail Marys . . Glory Be . . .O my Jesus . .

4. Jesus, You took Your Cross upon Your wounded shoulder and carried it patiently on the road to Calvary. You sacrificed Your way of the Cross for our salvation. You carried the heavy cross in order to heal us.

With this decade, I sacrifice to You all those, who have destroyed their spiritual, mental and physical health through drugs and alcohol and who have become ill, who need so much care and love, but are being rejected because no one accepts them. They are condemned to again carry their crosses in loneliness and are rejected by all. They became victims of their own behavior so that no one has compassion for them.

I ask You to have mercy on them and to heal them in spirit and soul. Send them Your Mother, Mary, to comfort them, as She comforted You. May there be good and compassionate people, like Simeon and Veronica, who will accept and help them to carry their heavy crosses and to wipe their disfigured faces. Bless all those, who are already doing this now.

Our Father . . 10 Hail Marys . . Glory Be . . .O my Jesus . .

5. I thank You, Jesus, for Your death on the Cross. I thank You because You forgave everyone and gave us Mary as our Mother and us to Her as Her children.

Have mercy on all victims of drugs and alcohol and all those, who have died from an overdose. Have mercy on those, who have killed addicts violently. May Your mercy deliver them. Give them the peace, which they had looked for in their addictions. Since everyone condemns them, do not condemn them!

They are victims of evil and sin, victims of those, for whom money has become their god. Invite all those into Your peace, who are now dying abandoned, forgotten and rejected by everyone. Be their comfort and strength in their last moments.

Mary, You became the Mother of us all, take on those, who have lost their lives in this way. Be an intercessor for the dead and a comfort for the living.

Our Father . . 10 Hail Marys . . Glory Be . . .O my Jesus . .

THE GLORIOUS MYSTERIES

Three days after Your death, You rose and comforted Your Mother and Your friends, who were weeping over You. Give me the grace to be able to enter already now into the secret of Your Resurrection. Send me Your Holy Spirit and let me and all those, who have died spiritually, participate in a new life.

Mary, because You have suffered with love, You were the first, who was worthy to experience the peace of Easter. May these Glorious mysteries of the Rosary, help me and all those, who are without peace, to enter into peace.

CREED

I beleive . . .

1. Frightened and weeping women were looking for You. You approached them and said, " Do not be afraid, It is I, peace be with you." Peace came back into their hearts.

Resurrected Lord, greet with Your peace of Easter, all who start today with unrest and who may become possible victims of drugs, alcohol and other addictions. Tell their hearts that they should not have any fear because You are living.

Our Father . . 10 Hail Marys . . Glory Be . . .O my Jesus . .

2. You blessed all those, who gathered on the mountain from which You ascended into heaven.

Bless us all today, especially the young, and may Your blessing protect them from every evil and sin, especially from addiction so that they will always remain free and will be able to live their life in dignity.

Our Father . . 10 Hail Marys . . Glory Be . . .O my Jesus . .

3. I thank You, Jesus, because You sent Your Holy Spirit over the apostles, who were praying with Mary.

I pray to You for the Church, the families and the authorities that, with the strength of Your Spirit, they will do everything to prevent the danger of drugs and so save all young people. Awaken all merciful hearts with Your Holy Spirit, may they answer courageously and help all, who are already victims of drugs or are in danger of becoming so.

Our Father . . 10 Hail Marys . . Glory Be . . .O my Jesus . .

4. Be blessed, Holy Father, because You preserved Mary from all evil and from every sin and because She always collaborated with Your holy will and was worthy to be assumed into heaven.

Through Her intercession, help all, who have become enslaved through sin and evil and have lost the dignity and sense for their life. May She, who was assumed into heaven, be their intercessor, their comfort and their new hope. May they, through Her intercession, discover new ways of life.

Our Father . . 10 Hail Marys . . Glory Be . . .O my Jesus . .

5. I thank You, heavenly Father, because You crowned Mary as Queen of heaven and earth.

I thank You for the hope of eternal life!

May She, our Queen, be the hope for us all to one day come to You to enjoy love and peace in Your eternal glory. May the eternal glory shine for us in the present darkness and be a beacon for us in this valley of suffering.

Our Father . . 10 Hail Marys . . Glory Be . . .O my Jesus . .

Final Prayer: I thank You, Jesus, I thank You, Mary, because I was able to spend this time with You in joy, sorrow and glory. May the Holy Spirit help me that I, while I meditate upon Your lives, become more similar to You in the Holy Spirit, who lives and reigns in eternity. Amen.

THE WAY OF THE CROSS FOR ADDICTS

(This prayer is meant as a prayer for addicts. At the beginning of the prayer, decide for whom you will pray and mention him by name in your prayer. Do not forget: an addict is not only a person, who takes drugs, but also a passionate smoker, an alcoholic, someone, who wastes time in front of video games, gambling, etc.)

Prayer of Preparation

Lord Jesus, You were completely free. You were only dependent on the will of the Father, which You accepted consciously in the Garden of Gethsemane. In Your freedom, You loved and sacrificed Your life for us with love. Today I want to be with You in Your suffering and I want to ask You for my personal freedom and love, and this I especially ask for................................. ....(mention the name of the person for whom you are praying). You know, Lord, that ....has lost his freedom and lives like a slave of drugs. (If it concerns another bad habit, mention it !) I believe

in Your love, with which You suffer for us and that is why I ask You, Jesus, believing that You give back freedom and love to all addicts, especially for ....

Send him the spirit of freedom and love so that he can overcome every enslavement. Pour out the spirit that gives life to bring him back from death. Pour out the spirit of strength so that he can overcome every weakness.

Mary, You also have freely accepted the will of the Father and have loved. Intercede today for all addicts, especially for ...., he is also Your child. Also for him, Your Son endured the bitter suffering and the bitter death. Through Your intercession, may he resurrect to a new life. May all works of the Spirit be resurrected in him and may all acts of the body, the world and darkness be conquered. Amen.

—*Have mercy on us, O Lord.*
—*Have mercy on us.*

Stood the mournful Mother weeping
At the Cross Her station keeping
Seeing Her Son crucified.

Holy Mother hear my prayers,
in my heart
renew each wound
of Jesus my Saviour.

FIRST STATION
JESUS, YOU ARE CONDEMNED TO DEATH

—*We adore You, O Christ, and we praise You*

—*because by Your holy Cross You have redeemed the world.*

Jesus, Pilate condemns You to death. He knows You are not guilty and he says solemnly in front of all that he cannot find any fault with You. Still he does not have the strength to protect You. He decides for injustice and untruth against You, the innocent one, because he is dependent.

His power and position are more important to him than truth and justice. He sacrifices You to save his position.

He has to act this way because he is dependent and has no freedom.

And You, Jesus, are free and that is why You can accept the condemnation and remain silent.

I thank You!

Jesus, I pray to You for the addict, whom You know and love. You know that he has also lost his freedom and is destroying himself. He is also ready to sacrifice everything and to lose everything in order to satisfy his dependencies. Give him back his freedom and give him the strength to free himself from his enslavement.

I pray to You also for all, who have become dependent on money, and ruthlessly distribute drugs to become richer. Free them! I pray to You for all those, who have offered the addicts a drug for the first time. Enlighten their minds and fill their hearts with freedom so that they will stop to do evil to others. I pray to You for all those responsible in the Church and in society so that they will be able to protect, in freedom, the freedom of others.

Give me the strength that, from now on, I will, with love fight courageously against any type of addiction.

Our Father, Hail Mary, Glory Be.

—*Have mercy on us, O Lord.*
—*Have mercy on us.*

Through Her heart, His sorrow sharing,
All His bitter anguish bearing,
Now at length the sword has passed.

Holy Mother hear my prayers,
in my heart
renew each wound
of Jesus my Saviour.

SECOND STATION
JESUS, YOU ACCEPT THE HEAVY CROSS

—We adore You, O Christ, and we praise You

—because by Your holy Cross You have redeemed the world.

Jesus, You accept Your Cross voluntarily and invite all, who want to be Yours, to accept their crosses and follow You. Your Cross, that You accept in freedom and love, becomes the Cross that redeems us because each suffering, which is accepted with love, teaches and redeems man.

I now offer You the suffering and the cross of this addict, which he has taken upon himself and which is destroying him as a human being and as a Christian. He accepted the cross at the moment when he believed the lies of those, who offered him drugs as a solution to his problems and when he accepted the drugs. I know that he is a victim and that he suffers much and that, through his addiction, he has put a cross upon his family, his parents and his friends. Now that cross, which consists of problems coming from the addiction, is upon our shoulders and that is why the disorder, not only came into his life, but into the life of us all.

Today I ask You for the strength for this addict so that he can discard the cross of addiction from his shoulders. I ask You for the strength that we can accept this suffering with patience, can forgive one another and so become Your students.

Our Father, Hail Mary, Glory Be.

—*Have mercy on us, O Lord.*
—*Have mercy on us.*

Oh how sad and sore distressed
Was that Mother highly blest
Of the sole-begotten Son.

Holy Mother hear my prayers,
in my heart
renew each wound
of Jesus my Saviour.

THIRD STATION
JESUS YOU FALL FOR THE FIRST TIME
BENEATH THE CROSS

—*We adore You, O Christ, and we praise You*

—*because by Your holy Cross You have redeemed the world.*

The Cross is heavy and Your strength wanes, the way up to Calvary is stony and this is why You fall under your Cross. You do not accuse the others, but You sacrifice this fall so that we can get up.

When we discovered the cross of addiction and saw that the addict, for whom I now pray, fell into the temptation of narcotics and fatal drugs; we also, in his environment, fell into impatience and hopelessness, lost love and faith and accused one another. The cross of disorder becomes too heavy and suffocates the understanding for one another. We accuse him and each other.

Give us the grace so that we do not sink deeper, but courageously and wisely, offer each other, our hands to rise again. I ask You also for the families, who do not yet know that the fall into the drug is seriously threatening them. Give them the grace to discover the evil in time so that the fall will not come about.

Our Father, Hail Mary, Glory Be.

—Have mercy on us, O Lord.
—Have mercy on us.

Is there one who would not weep,
Whelmed in miseries so deep
Christ's dear Mother to behold?

Holy Mother hear my prayers,
in my heart
renew each wound
of Jesus my Saviour.

FOURTH STATION
JESUS, YOU MEET YOUR HOLY MOTHER

—We adore You, O Christ, and we praise You

—because by Your holy Cross You have redeemed the world.

The meeting between You, Jesus and Your Mother, is a drop of comfort in the ocean of condemnation, bitterness, violence, threats and insults for both of You. Someone who loves can meet others and, through the meeting, give strength and alleviate the pain. Thank You for this meeting, which gives hope to us all. You know, Jesus, that many people can no longer meet in love. Especially there, where there are drugs, one avoids meeting, one does not talk to one another, one runs away and is afraid of the other.

How sad is the situation in the families, where parents do not meet their children because children avoid the meeting! How difficult is the situation for the children there, where father and mother have no time for them! So the way opens for the fatal addiction.

Now I pray to You, Jesus together with Mary, that You give this addict the strength that he can meet the persons, with whom he is living, in truth, love and without fear; give them the strength so that they will be ready for this meeting, so that he can free himself from the fatal embrace of drugs and find his way back into the life-giving embrace of his parents and of us all, who live with him.

I offer to You, Jesus, also the first meeting with the person, who had supplied him with the drug and I pray for this person. Heal the wounds and make us able to meet each other with love and with truth.

Our Father, Hail Mary, Glory Be.

—*Have mercy on us, O Lord.*
—*Have mercy on us.*

Can the human heart refrain
From partaking in Her pain,
In that Mother's pain untold?

Holy Mother hear my prayers,
in my heart
renew each wound
of Jesus my Saviour.

FIFTH STATION
JESUS, SIMON THE CYRENE
HELPS YOU CARRY THE CROSS

—We adore You, O Christ, and we praise You

—because by Your holy Cross You have redeemed the world.

Jesus, You say that we are not being tempted beyond our strength. Here is a man, who accepts Your Cross willingly and carries it for You because he sees Your exhaustion and Your suffering. You are thankful to him.

I admit, Jesus, that we are blind for one another. This addict carried the cross of his sufferings, got up exhausted; he lost the will to live, to work and we, around him, saw all that, but did not take notice of it. Had there been a good Simon at the right moment, the cross of this addict would surely not have been so heavy.

I pray to You to make Simons out of me and all people who will see and, in seeing, will know how to help.

I thank You today for all those, who recognize addicts, feel their sufferings and help them to free themselves. Give us all the graces so that we are not afraid to help those who need our help.

Our Father, Hail Mary, Glory Be.

—Have mercy on us, O Lord.
—Have mercy on us.

Who could see that Mother's grief
without being saddened too,
While She suffers with Her Son?

Holy Mother hear my prayers,
in my heart

renew each wound
of Jesus my Saviour.

SIXTH STATION
JESUS, VERONICA OFFERS YOU
HER VEIL AND WIPES YOUR FACE

—*We adore You, O Christ, and we praise You*

—*because by Your holy Cross You have redeemed the world.*

All see Your disfigured face but there is nobody, except the courageous woman Veronica, who approaches You to wipe the sweat and blood from Your face. She does that. She knows that she will be given scornful looks when she will do something good for You. That does not bother her. She courageously approaches You and accomplishes her merciful act. You leave an imprint of Your face on her veil and so show how thankful You are.

Jesus, how many times has the addict shown his pale, blank face and his bloodshot eyes in front of my eyes and the eyes of his parents and we did not see it and did not know how to approach him how to talk to him and how to help him.

I thank You today for Sister Elvira and all those, who recognize the disfigured faces of addicts, and who do everything to help them. I pray to You for the grace for us all, so that we can recognize them in time and help in the right way.

I pray to You for the grace of confession for all, who have become addicts. May confession be a meeting for them with You and may it help them to free themselves.

Our Father, Hail Mary, Glory Be.

—*Have mercy on us, O Lord.*
—*Have mercy on us.*

For the sins of all the people
Saw Jesus hang in desolation,
All with bloody scourges rent.

Holy Mother hear my prayers,
in my heart
renew each wound
of Jesus my Saviour.

SEVENTH STATION
JESUS, YOU FALL
THE SECOND TIME BENEATH THE CROSS

—We adore You, O Christ, and we praise You

—because by Your holy Cross You have redeemed the world.

On Your way, You fall for the second time under Your too-heavy Cross. The second fall is more difficult than the first. It is more difficult to get up again after the second fall than the first. And still You get up.

I thank You because You consistently do the will of the Father.

Jesus, You know how many times addicts decide not to take anymore drugs, promise this to their parents and friends, but cannot keep their word because the evil of addiction is stronger than their good will. With the renewed fall, many lose the courage and do not try to get up again. No one believes them anymore, because they have so often promised not to take anymore drugs but then have taken them again; that is, they fell again.

I pray to You for this addict and all addicts that they-in spite of the new fall-will not lose hope and will go on courageously. Send them the people, who will help them.

With Your force, stop all those, who through selling drugs, cause the renewed falls of those, who have become weak.

Our Father, Hail Mary, Glory Be.

—Have mercy on us, O Lord.
—Have mercy on us.

See this most beloved Son,
dying there in desolation
Till His Spirit forth He sent.

Holy Mother hear my prayers,
in my heart
renew each wound
of Jesus my Saviour.

EIGHTH STATION
JESUS, YOU CONSOLE
THE WEEPING WOMEN OF JERUSALEM

—We adore You, O Christ, and we praise You

—because by Your holy Cross You have redeemed the world.

Your pain does not enclose You within Yourself. You notice the women on the side of the road, who have compassion for You. In spite of Your sufferings, You do not forget Your mission and this is why You invite the women-the mothers-to conversion and so announce the moment of salvation to them. Through their conversion, they will save themselves, their families and their people. You tell them clearly that they will perish if they do not convert.

Today, I pray to You for the parents of this addict, may they also convert and with their conversion, help his conversion and liberation from the addiction. I pray to You also for all parents and teachers of the young so that, with their conversion, they can protect their children and the young.

May also those, who distribute drugs among the young and who enrich themselves at the expense of their ruin, hear the invitation for conversion and stop inflicting evil upon others.

I pray to You for all those responsible in society and in the Church so that they will become active in the fight against every type of addiction. Forgive us all because we neither hear the invitation to change our life nor do we change.

Our Father, Hail Mary, Glory Be.

—Have mercy on us, O Lord.
—Have mercy on us.

May the flame of my own heart,
Love Jesus Your Son,
So that I please Him.

Holy Mother hear my prayers,
in my heart
renew each wound
of Jesus my Saviour.

NINTH STATION
JESUS, YOU FALL
THE THIRD TIME BENEATH THE CROSS

—We adore You, O Christ, and we praise You

—because by Your holy Cross You have redeemed the world.

You stumble again and fall and are lying under Your Cross. Those, who are torturing You, are again happy when they see Your misery. In their arrogance, they delight in Your renewed fall. With Your remaining strength, You get up and continue Your way and again carry Your heavy Cross with dignity.

I pray to You, Jesus, for this addict, who has promised so many times that he will stop to destroy himself and us, but who has fallen again. We do not delight in his falls but we did condemn and reject him. Forgive us and may all forgive us, whom we have condemned.

I pray to You also for those, who have completely destroyed their health and who have lost their inner freedom and will try to again. Give them the grace that they will try again with their remaining strength and that they will succeed. I offer to You also those, who are endangered today to take an overdose of drugs and to end their difficult life in this way. Have mercy also on them, may Your Spirit of strength fill them, so that they can free themselves from the embrace of death and can begin a life in freedom again.

Our Father, Hail Mary, Glory Be.

—Have mercy on us, O Lord.
—Have mercy on us.

Thy Son in torment on the Cross,
Who for me was crucified
Let me share with Thee His pain.

Holy Mother hear my prayers,
in my heart
renew each wound
of Jesus my Saviour.

TENTH STATION
JESUS, YOU ARE
STRIPPED OF YOUR GARMENTS

—*We adore You, O Christ, and we praise You*

—*because by Your holy Cross You have redeemed the world.*

Jesus, I see how they cause You a further pain. They strip You of Your garments, over which they will throw dice. You are totally poor and are exposed to the eyes of the people. Your heart and Your soul, however, are full of love and peace. They cannot make You spiritually poor because, also at this moment, You are divinely rich and use it to show the strength of Your love.

Jesus, each addict and also the one, for whom I am especially praying today, is poor and has made his family poor. He sold everything from the house that he could sell. He stole and made many debts, deceiving people by telling them he will return everything. The parents are helpless. The situation is difficult, but it is even more serious that his soul has become completely poor. There remains only a terrible emptiness on the inside and on the outside.

I pray to You, Jesus, heal his soul and his heart, give him the inner wealth of love, faith, hope, sincerity and honesty, love of truth and give him the will to live a life in openness and peace. I pray to You also for those, who have enriched themselves with the poverty of the addicts.

Free them from their greed and give them the grace to respect each life and material goods. Many have fallen ill with the terrible sickness of AIDS and other contagious diseases because of a loss of dignity on the moral level. They also kill conceived children. Many children are infected and are born already ill and so their life is being made more difficult.

Have mercy on all, heal them and give them back their original dignity, with which the Father, the Creator, has enriched every soul.

Our Father, Hail Mary, Glory Be.

—Have mercy on us, O Lord
—Have mercy on us.

Let me mingle tears with thee,
For Jesus dear, beloved,
All the days that I may live.

Holy Mother hear my prayers,
in my heart
renew each wound
of Jesus my Saviour.

ELEVENTH STATION
JESUS, YOU ARE
BEING NAILED TO THE CROSS

—We adore You, O Christ, and we praise You

—because by Your holy Cross You have redeemed the world.

The hatred transforms itself into violence and is being poured over You. With nails, they pierce Your hands and feet. This is also a moment, in which Your immeasureable love shows itself, because You accept to be crucified for us in order to save us.

Jesus, the addict for whom I pray, is filled with the spirit of violence against himself and others. He crucifies himself, his spiritual, mental and physical health. He crucifies his parents and his relatives on the same cross. He is violent against old and helpless people just to obtain money.

Jesus, You know that today many suffer because of their addiction, they either endure violence or they are violent themselves. I offer them to You and pray that You will free them from the spirit of violence, hate and deception.

Free the families of addicts from violence and destruction, may they be filled with the spirit of mildness, goodness, peace, mutual forgiveness and understanding. Stop all those hands, who distribute deadening means to others and all who take them, so that each life will be saved.

Our Father, Hail Mary, Glory Be.

—Have mercy on us, O Lord.
—Have mercy on us.

Virgin of all virgins blest!
Listen to my fond request:
Let me share Thy grief divine.

Holy Mother hear my prayers,
in my heart
renew each wound
of Jesus my Saviour.

TWELFTH STATION
JESUS, YOU ARE
DYING ON THE CROSS FOR US

— We adore You, O Christ, and we praise You

—because by Your holy Cross You have redeemed the world.

Jesus, You are dying on the Cross. You forgive and pray for those, who have done violence unto You. You have become the victim in order to save us. You do not forget Your Mother and Your disciple, but express Your last wish-that they accept each other.

I bring You now all victims of drugs, alcohol and violence that result from addiction. Have mercy on them, welcome them into Your kingdom. Have mercy also on those, who in hopeless situations, have taken their own lives and those, who were driving under the influence of drugs and brought death unto themselves and others. May their death also be an invitation to all addicts to make a decision for life. Invite all those into Your kingdom of peace, who die now from an overdose. May no one be lost forever.

(Remain in silence for sometime and pray with your own words!)

Our Father, Hail Mary, Glory Be.

—Have mercy on us, O Lord.
—Have mercy on us.

Let me be wounded with His wounds
Be saturated with His Cross,
And with the blood of Your dear Son.

Holy Mother hear my prayers,
in my heart
renew each wound
of Jesus my Saviour.

THIRTEENTH STATION
JESUS, YOU ARE TAKEN DOWN
FROM THE CROSS AND YOU ARE PLACED
IN THE EMBRACE OF YOUR MOTHER

—We adore You, O Christ, and we praise You

—because by Your holy Cross You have redeemed the world.

Mary, I thank You because You endure to suffer courageously with Your Son. I thank You because Your love and faith are not being broken. You are sad, but have not lost hope. And while You hold Your dead Son in Your lap, You are similar to all parents, who have lost a child because of an addiction. They are similar to You in the sorrow but, in their sadness, they have lost faith and hope and, also often, the will to work and the will for life. Welcome them, Mary, and help them so that they will receive again love and hope.

I bring to You all young addicts so that You can protect them in Your motherly embrace from the evil of addiction. I also bring You all those, who are in danger of becoming addicts. Protect them and send them people, who will be a help to them on the way to freedom.

Our Father, Hail Mary, Glory Be.

—Have mercy on us, O Lord.
—Have mercy on us.

Be to me, O Virgin, nigh,
Lest in flames I burn and die.
In His awful Judgement day.

Holy Mother hear my prayers,
in my heart
renew each wound
of Jesus my Saviour.

FOURTEENTH STATION
JESUS, YOU ARE
PLACED INTO THE TOMB

—We adore You, O Christ, and we praise You

—because by Your holy Cross You have redeemed the world.

Jesus, You are being placed into the tomb. It seems as if everything is over. But for You, this is the moment, in which You are nearest to the glory of the Resurrection. Mary's heart feels this also, while She and Her friends sadly are putting You into the tomb.

Bless all graves of addicts and all places where they spend their last moments. Bless all families, who accompany today a victim of drugs to his last resting-place. May the belief in enternal life be their strength.

Give us all, who are still on our way, the grace to live so that we will be worthy to reach Your kingdom. Amen.

Our Father, Hail Mary, Glory Be.

—Have mercy on us, O Lord.
—Have mercy on us.

While my body here decays,
May my soul Thy goodness praise,
With Your glory forever!

Holy Mother hear my prayers,
in my heart
renew each wound
of Jesus my Saviour.

THE PRAYER IN FRONT OF THE CROSS

We adore Your Cross because it is a sign of Your love. With the power of Your most precious blood, cleanse us from all sin and protect us from every influence of Satan. May the river of peace and reconciliation flow from this site into the hearts of all people.

May all addicts look upon the Cross with faith and be healed from the poison of drugs, as those were healed, who were looking with faith at the sign, which Moses had raised in front of their eyes in the desert.

In the name of all addicts, who have no faith, I meditate on Your Cross and pray that You will heal them in body and soul, that You free them and give them the love for life.

May Your Cross always invite us and encourage us to give, with love, our life for each other in freedom. Amen.

SUMMARY: AFTERTHOUGHTS AND SUGGESTIONS

It seems important to me to explain once more briefly the most important points, concerning problems of addiction and addicts, and to show possible actions, with which we can responsibly resist this terrible virus of our day.

1. SO THAT WE ARE WELL OR SO THAT WE BECOME GOOD

It is a fact that every person would like to feel well and to feel well is connected with pleasure and the feeling of contentment. A deep need for the satisfaction of pleasurable feelings is in itself the basis from where addiction originates. But pleasure in itself is blind, therefore, it must be guided by the intellect and the will. When a wish for pleasure becomes a passion, then that happens what should never happen to a person-he surrenders everything for the satisfaction of his desires. The situation, in which a person finds himself today, especially the young, corresponds in no way with the development of the whole person. All possibilities, that man has created for himself in the area of technology and the stimulation of his cravings, are particularly dangerous for the development of the human personality. When one fulfills all the wishes of a child and does everything so that he is well, but forgets that one must also strive for the child to become good, then the first severe break in the person occurs. Thus, the person becomes spiritually and mentally lazy and looks for the easiest ways for him to feel well and be well. At the same time, he loses patience and has no strength to fight in order to be good. And so he gives in.

A person can only appreciate and protect those things for which he has fought in his life and which he has attained with his own strength through renunciation, sacrifice and efforts.

Therefore, it is clear that when a child is used to having everything at once, what the parents have earned with great effort, then that child does not appreciate the work of the parents because he neither sees them nor is with them often. The child develops into a real 'terrorist' against his father and mother until he gets what he wants.

If we want to establish a rule for life out of this, then it should be as follows:

Give the child everything he needs and teach him, according to your experiences, that everything is a fruit of efforts and sufferings of a person. Do not allow the child to easily obtain unnecessary things and do not fulfill his every wish in order to calm him. Because, if one begins to give the child more and more in order to calm and satisfy him, one begins a dangerous and endless game which leads into destruction.

Specifically, this concerns TV programs, the choice of what one hears and sees, sweets, food, toys,…one must have strict control over everything and accompany the child in his growth.

2. EVERYONE IS A POSSIBLE ADDICT

Aside from the entire tragedy of addiction, we must also recognize the frightening possiblity that everyone can become an addict because man, according to his nature, is addicted to something. The question is only how one learns to control the need for pleasure. I dare to say that there is no family or education so ideal that it can exclude the fall into addiction. But this should, however, not discourage us, just as a possible car accident does not discourage us to buy a car, to go out onto the street and to drive in traffic. A possible accident must not frighten us but make us a careful and attentive driver. Both drivers are not always responsible for the accident.

In other words, according to his nature and without a genuine responsibility for others, for the parents, the teachers, society, any person can become an addict. This is an internal factor that is inborn in every person. But, as far as drugs are concerned, there is a dangerous external factor. There are organized persons who distribute drugs. These are those 'friends' of the young, who told them for the first time, "take it, try it once, it is not dangerous!" Surely there are also those, who have tried it and gave it up again. This is what those expect, who at first offer the drugs at no cost; but they know that there is always a large percentage of those, who have tried and will also continue to use it and so become a serious and regular customer of their fatal goods.

In this manner, the drug dealers earn drugs or money for themselves, which have become their god, for whom they are ready to sacrifice everything. In their addiction to drugs or money, they are tirelessly active and this is why they are so successful.

Drug addicts are in extreme solidarity with each other so that they are ready to do anything for each other. It is also well known that they kill each other, if someone tries to break their chain either through elimination or through becoming an 'informant' for the police.

Especially at the present time, we feel the situation of the drugs like a horrific storm, which we helplessly face and are not capable of doing anything about. There, where such a situation arises, drugs find an opened door and are free to act.

It is clear to us that for non-addicts there are no clear guide lines to prevent all this. But this does not mean that they do not exist. I am convinced that-according to the law of resistence of life against death-something is born in the living and that they will find the right means to protect themselves against this disaster.

3. BE ACTIVE

It is true that we cannot stop a storm that destroys everything in front of it; but man has an umbrella, a raincoat and has built a home and, in this manner, protects himself from the damage of the storm. I am convinced that one can do something immediately.

I. The parents should be the first to act. They have to watch their child consciously and attentively, but also watch what is happening around the child. They have to take a courageous, clear, loud, and tireless stand against addiction.

For this purpose, I suggest that parent associations be started, in which they will be in solidarity and which enable them to attentively watch over their children and call the behavior of their children to each other's attention.

(I remember one case when I asked parents, who had just discovered the addiction of their child, to tell other parents that their child was taking drugs; but they were not prepared to do this, because they were afraid of the reactions of the others. Their reaction is always a disaster because parents cannot reconcile themselves with the fact that their child is taking drugs!)

The parent associations in Ireland can serve as an example to us. Mothers and fathers have gotten together and organized themselves, they 'patrol' their village and so prevent the expansion of drugs. This is an example one should think about!

II. The second suggestion is that priests or schools organize youth groups, who will be taught and made able to follow peers and to protect them from the drugs. They are best able to do this because they know the behavior of their colleagues better than anyone else.

There is much that one can do. For us, one example can be the Franciscans in Humac near Ljubuški, who, during Lent in 1997, suggested to the parish that they **pray and fast** in order to prevent the spreading of drugs. Many people, many families and youth groups have accepted this proposal and have begun to pray and fast for these intentions. In addition to prayer and fasting and homilies about the same topic, meetings were organized with healed addicts from the community of Sister Elvira in Medjugorje and experts of addictions. This is an example that invites other activities.

Also state institutions, especially the police, should be constantly made aware of the situation and they should be asked to help in the fight against addiction and in breaking its chains.

4. WITH TRUTH AGAINST THE ENDLESS LIE

An addict is, first of all, a victim of a lie. At the beginning, a friend tells him that it is not dangerous. He knowingly lies to him and makes him a victim of the lie. According to the logic of events, from a lie only a lie can be born. First they are dishonest to themselves, then to their parents, to the family and in school.

This is also one of the signs with which one recognizes an addict. But so that the parents can discover the lie, they must be alert and in continuous contact with their children, with the school and the professor of religion. Jesus said that the truth would set us free, so it is important to continuously inform oneself and to spread the truth about the consequences of drugs for the soul, the spirit and the body.

Drugs kill the gifts of the spirit and activate the works of the flesh. St. Paul writes, "Now the works of the flesh are obvious: immorality, impurity, licentiousness, idolatry, sorcery, hatreds, rivalry, jealousy, outbursts of fury, acts of selfishness, dissensions, factions, occasions of envy, drinking bouts, orgies, and the like. I warn you, as I warned you before, that those who do such things will not inherit the kingdom of God.

In contrast, the fruit of the Spirit is love, joy, peace, patience, kindness, generosity, faithfulness, gentleness and self-control." (Gal. 5, 19-22)

Therefore, one must fight with the spirit against the flesh and the world.

5. THE BEGINNING OF VIOLENCE AND THEFT

It is very expensive to be addicted. One has to obtain the money. So begins theft in the home and when there is nothing more left in the home to steal, then one steals also outside the home. First one steals things, which are the easiest to sell. And when this does not bring enough money for one day, then one begins to break-in there, where one suspects money is and continues with being violent against people. There is no choice. Anyone, who is a possible source of money, is attacked.

6. PSYCHO/PHYSICAL CONSEQUENCES

Different drugs have a different effect on the health of the soul and body. In short, drugs lead to deep psychoses, which cause all types of mental illnesses, destroy the physical health; but most endangered are the brain, the blood vessels, the kidneys, the liver and the heart.

In the complete healings in the communities, they succeed in regaining the spiritual health and also, in many cases, the physical health; but the most serious consequences of drugs remain in the mental health of the person.

All consequences in the soul, spirit and body invite us in the same degree to be active and to save the person at any cost. When we have saved one single person, we have saved the family and the entire society from the terrible consequences of the fatal drugs and this is worth it! One must only love life!

CONSECRATION PRAYER TO OUR LADY

(This consecration prayer is being prayed by the youths in the community at the end of each morning prayer!)

In awareness of my Christian mission, I .... put my baptismal pledge into Your hands, Mary: I withstand Satan, I withstand drugs, I withstand all evil, all his temptations and all his works and I consecrate myself to Jesus Christ to faithfully carry my cross with Him each day, according to the will of God. In the presence of the Church, I accept You, Mary, as my Mother and Empress. I consecrate to You my person, my life and the value of all my good deeds; the past, the present and the future. Direct me and everything that belongs to me to the greater glory of God for all time and in eternity. Amen.

Publisher:

INFORMATIVNI ✝ CENTAR

mir

M E Đ U G O R J E

internet: http://www.medjugorje.hr
e-mail: medjugorje-mir@medjugorje.hr

For the publisher:
fra Miljenko Stojić

Technical editor:
Emil Kordić

Edition: 3000 copies

Printing finished in February 1998.

Printed by: **GRAF✪TISAK**